# Teaching and Learning
# Outside the Box

# Teaching and Learning Outside the Box

*Inspiring Imagination Across The Curriculum*

EDITED BY

KIERAN EGAN
MAUREEN STOUT
KEIICHI TAKAYA

Teachers College
Columbia University
New York and London

Published by Teachers College Press, 1234 Amsterdam Avenue, New York, NY 10027

*Library of Congress Cataloging-in-Publication Data*

Teaching and learning outside the box : inspiring imagination across the curriculum / edited by Kieran Egan, Maureen Stout, and Keiichi Takaya.
    p.  cm.
  Includes bibliographical references and index.
  ISBN 978-0-8077-4781-0 (pbk. : alk. paper)
  ISBN 978-0-8077-4782-7 (cloth : alk. paper)
  1. Educational psychology. 2. Imagination. I. Egan, Kieran. II. Stout, Maureen.
III. Takaya, Keiichi.
  LB1062.T4 2007
  370.15—dc22

                                           2006102011

ISBN 978-0-8077-4781-0 (paper)
ISBN 978-0-8077-4782-7 (cloth)

Printed on acid-free paper

Manufactured in the United States of America

14  13  12  11  10 09 08 07     8  7  6  5  4  3  2  1

# Contents

# Preface

Imagination is an essential aspect of education and helps us improve teaching and learning by allowing us to see the world in new ways. In *Teaching and Learning Outside the Box: Inspiring Imagination Across the Curriculum* we explore these new perspectives on education through a variety of lenses—historical, philosophical, social, and psychological, to name a few—while examining the role and import of imagination in public education.

We believe that schools must nurture and develop students' intellectual, moral, and aesthetic imaginations, to ensure successful and meaningful educational experiences. However, all too often, lessons and activities fail to stimulate crucial aspects of students' imaginations, despite instructional programs that appear to employ imaginative materials and methods. Multimedia presentations, for example, are employed in almost all subjects but may do little to enhance imagination. In our view, this is because current principles and methods are based on a somewhat superficial understanding of the importance of imagination in students' lives. In this book we aim to deepen that understanding and establish the practical and theoretical significance of imagination in education.

Kieran Egan's introductory chapter provides an overview of the importance of imagination in education, while the authors in Part I view the concept of imagination from several historical and philosophical perspectives. The contributors to Part II address some prevalent myths regarding imagination, explore how imagination is a foundational part of learning, and illustrate how imaginative education can look in practice.

Some of the chapters contain particular interpretations of the connection between imagination and education, while others challenge some common myths and misunderstandings regarding the role of imagination in teaching and learning. One prevalent myth, for example, is that science has nothing to do with imagination; another is that imagination is the prerogative of the arts. The authors attempt to "demythify" imagination by examining these myths and by illustrating the importance of imagination in these fields.

In *The Educated Mind, Imagination in Teaching and Learning* and other books, Professor Egan has explained that stimulating students' imaginative capacities is a vital educational end and that it is central to making instructional activities effective and meaningful for all students. However, despite his and others' findings, and despite current initiatives promoting imaginative teaching and learning in schools, there has been no systematic attempt to examine why and how the concept of imagination is important in education. Such an understanding is essential if we are to identify and implement ways to stimulate teachers' and students' imaginations not only to improve skill and knowledge acquisition, but also to transform the entire educational experience. We hope that *Teaching and Learning Outside the Box* may help us all take the first step in that transformation.

*Part I*

# Setting the Context for Imagination in Education

*Chapter 1*

# Imagination, Past and Present

## KIERAN EGAN

In different times and cultures, we human beings have characterized our mental capacities and functions in various ways. Today many scholars are still trying to work out just what the ancient Greeks meant by the array of labels they gave to those functions. One feature of our minds that is recognized by all cultures is the imagination. Everyone recognizes a capacity that allows us to call up mental images, think about things that are not present, or consider things that do not exist. Not everyone has labeled imagination in the same way or has the same beliefs and feelings about it, but it is something that is universally recognized.

As an introduction to the chapters that follow, I wish to explore some of the meanings of imagination in the Western tradition—the tradition that has shaped the sense of the term most commonly used today in Western countries, and increasingly in other cultures too. I examine how imagination has been characterized over the past few millennia to help us understand its meaning and purpose in education today.

Studying imagination is not like studying science in a couple of important ways. First, of course, we tend to have a better and clearer sense of what science is, if only because it is a cultural artifact of our own invention. This doesn't mean that science is an uncontested concept, or that it doesn't reflect features of our mental operations. Second, the story we might tell about science is clearly a progressive one; modern science is better than ancient or medieval or early-modern science. This doesn't mean that we have brighter people doing science today, just that the methodologies are much better elaborated and the results of applying those methodologies are more effective. It is far from clear that we could tell a similar story about the imagination. It is far from clear that we are better imaginers than were our hunter-gatherer ancestors long ago—in fact the opposite looks at first blush more likely.

Having looked briefly at how layers of meaning have been rolled through the centuries into what we call the imagination, I want to consider the possible uses of this capacity in education. In general, imagination has

*3*

not fared as well as might have been expected in educational writings about the design of curricula, teaching methods, and studies of students' learning. It seems to have become sidelined by agendas that are more urgent, that seek specific social objectives from teaching, and that focus on efficiency and accountability. From the perspective of those who have encouraged and directed this general movement in public education, imagination seems something of a frill; containing value, no doubt, but a value left to "the arts" rather than to the more central purposes of a public system that is paid for by people who often have objectives for their investment in mind that are more specific.

I want to argue that attention to the imagination is a better means to achieve the ends desired by those who currently direct public schooling; that the sidelined and neglected "frill" is actually the most effective tool we have for efficient and effective learning. The drive for improved test scores is commonly seen as incompatible with developing students' imaginations. I will argue that increased focus on students' imaginations will lead to improvements in all measures of educational achievement.

## SENSES OF IMAGINATION

Perhaps it should be no surprise that the paymasters of our public schools should have always been wary of imagination. It is a concept that has come down to us with a history of suspicion and distrust. Two of the main intellectual traditions that have shaped the Western understanding of the world have similar stories about imagination. The Hebrew Bible first uses a term that seems best translated as "imagination" in recounting the story of the building of the Tower of Babel. Jehovah said, "Behold the people, how nothing will be restrained from them, from what they have imagined to do" (Gen. 11:6, King James Version). The human imagination was the instrument identified as responsible for the impious human attempt to encroach on God's prerogatives. The punishment was the babel, or babble, of mutually incomprehensible languages. The ancient Greeks told the related story of Prometheus, who stole fire from the gods and gave it to humans. The possession of fire empowered humans in ways that, again, encroached on what had been the prerogatives of the gods. Prometheus—*pro-metheus* means "fore-thinker"—was punished by being chained to a rock and left to a very nasty fate.

In both the Hebrew and the Greek stories, humans' uses of imagination threaten to disturb their proper relationship with the divine and with the established order of things. The capacity to plan ahead by imagining possibilities that do not exist, is dangerous—a threat not only to gods but to human authorities too. Dictators have tended not to be at all pleased to see signs of imagination in their subjects.

Plato regarded the imagination as an inferior part of the mind (Conford, 1941). The most valuable intellectual function, which his educational program was designed to develop, was reason. Succumbing to the appeal of images, as opposed to abstract concepts, strengthened the lower functions of our minds at the expense of the higher, he thought, and provided a constant seductive counterpressure against the hard struggle for rationality, which alone disclosed to us the truth about reality. All images that human beings could make, by painting or sculpture, were, at best, merely copies of the original creative acts of the gods, and as the gods made reality, all copies and images must be inadequate and misleading in one way or another. However we interpret Plato's conclusion that poets and makers of original rhythms should be banned from his ideal society, it is clear that he bequeathed to us another powerful caveat about the value of the human imagination. Added to its dangers in leading us beyond our proper bounds was the further likelihood that its stimulation came at the expense of developing reason, and its seductive images would always lead us away from or to the side of what was real and true.

Plato's immensely influential construction of an image of our minds has imparted to us a sense of the imagination as being in some kind of conflict with reason. Their struggle is a zero-sum game; the more you have of one, the less you have of the other. It is no wonder that throughout history, educators, committed to the development of reason, have been nervous of what they have seen as its shadowy antagonist.

Aristotle articulated a rather more complex view of the imagination (Roberts, 1954). He did not so much displace the earlier distrust, or suggest that imagination was anything other than a mimetic, or copying, faculty as argue that it did perform an important intellectual function. Believing that all ideas began as sensations, that the baby who had no ideas became an adult full of ideas, left the problem of how sensations were converted into ideas—how world-stuff became mind-stuff. This transformation, Aristotle proposed, was wrought by the imagination.

During the European Middle Ages we find a now familiar distrust of the imagination, combined with the Aristotelian sense of it being potentially a useful intellectual servant—as long as it was kept under careful, that is reasonable, control. The problem with imagination, in most medieval writing about it, was the recognition that it was an untrustworthy servant, constantly threatening to become altogether too uppity. The imagination can be useful if it carries the mind towards God, but it must be constantly and firmly restrained by reason or it will more likely carry the mind and soul in the opposite direction. Its Aristotelian role as mediator between perception and ideas remains prominent, but here too it is a particularly weak and fallible part of intellectual activity, susceptible to confusing with reality the images it generates. This area of susceptibility is precisely the ideal stomping ground for the Devil. So, again, the imagination is not to be trusted; it is to be kept under the ever-vigilant control of reason.

The early Enlightenment did little to elevate the importance of the imagination. Descartes (1596–1650) considered it a source of confusion and "blundering constructions" that can only get in the way of the reason's analysis. This aggressive rationalism, along with the beginnings of scientific inquiry, saw the imagination as little other than a regrettable defect in our makeup: the cause of people having such difficulty seeing what was real and true without distortions. If it was granted any positive role at all, it was as a faculty that could produce an unserious pleasure or charm in the arts; a faculty of value for the idle hours when the mind's serious work was done and light entertainment was in order. These are very much the terms in which the protoscientist Francis Bacon (1561–1626) talks of it, and also, later, the literary man Joseph Addison (1672–1719). Their sense of "fancy" still hovers around our sense of imagination.

Into the 18th century the constructive role of the imagination was conceived to be very limited. Its ability to generate novelty, such as images of flying horses, was seen as relatively insignificant. From perception we derived images of horses, and also of wings; these could be put together in the mind. There was nothing particularly significant in this, it was suggested dismissively. The imagination was assumed to be incapable of producing anything absolutely new; it simply reordered ideas that it received from the senses. And in general it should be discouraged from this reordering, its most evident facility, because it threatened to undermine reason and its hold on reality.

A significant new role was suggested for the imagination by two leading philosophers of the later Enlightenment. David Hume (1711–1776) and Immanuel Kant (1724–1804) both conceived of the imagination as being crucial to our ability to construct a coherent view of the world. Hume saw it not simply as converting sense impressions into ideas, but as taking fleeting, partial, constantly shifting sense impressions and delivering from these to the mind a coherent and stable view of the world. Kant went a step further, suggesting that the imagination even structured our perceptions, so that what we can perceive and can know is predetermined by our imagination.

These scholars implicated the imagination in the most basic levels of human meaning-making. It should be noted that the empiricist Hume acknowledged this role of imagination with some reluctance, calling it "a kind of magical faculty" (Hume, 1739/1888, p. 24), and Kant later greatly reduced the significance he had earlier attached to it. Both, that is, ascribed to imagination functions that were required by their models of how knowledge was constructed, functions that remained mysterious. Even though they suggested an enlarged role for the imagination, it was hardly one that was easily understood.

The modern sense of the imagination as a productive, generative capacity comes very largely from the Romantics. In his *Biographia Literaria* (chap. 13), Coleridge declares, "The primary imagination I hold to be the living power and prime agent of all human perception and as a repetition in the finite mind of the eternal act of creation of the infinite I AM."

Here, for sure, is a conception of imagination that is significantly different from anything that had preceded it. The difference is in the emphasis laid on its creative, generative power. The Romantics also absorbed what has been called Kant's "Copernican Revolution." Just as Copernicus had shown that the Earth orbited the Sun, and not vice versa, so Kant showed that the nature of the human mind determined how the world was perceived; it did not simply reproduce an image of reality delivered by the senses.

The mind was thus conceived as less a mirror of a clear reality than a lamp onto a dark and complex reality (Abrams, 1958). The imagination was seen as so central to the process of making sense of the world that the Romantics attacked the claim that science was the one reliable path to uncovering the truth. The imaginative artist, they asserted, disclosed truth and reality no less, and in fact more profoundly, than the scientist: "Beauty is Truth, Truth Beauty," as John Keats compactly put it.

The Romantics, however, commonly overstated what was possible through the arts; they dealt, after all, in images rather than the material world. As Kearney (1988) deflatingly observes the "Romantic imagination could not possibly deliver on its promises" (p. 185), and as W. H. Auden concluded, "Poetry makes nothing happen" ("In Memory of W. B. Yeats," 1936). Romanticism elevated the imagination, but in the process continued to accept an image of the mind that set the imagination in opposition to or in conflict with rationality. While Wordsworth recognized that imagination is nothing other than "Reason in her most exalted mood" (1805/1991, bk. 14, line 192)—that the imagination is not some distinct faculty that operates separately from reason—too many Romantic artists identified the scientific mind, and the Industrial Revolution, which they saw as its product, as the enemy. So they passed down to us a conception of imagination that implied hostility to rationality.

This hasty gallop through the centuries has suggested some of the constituents of our current conception of imagination. We have certainly inherited the persistent sense of the imagination as being, at least, not a comfortable ally of reason in our minds. While a number of people support the view expressed in Wordsworth's words cited above—of imagination being simply reason working at its most effective—that view is making slow headway against the commoner, and cruder, notion of their being competitors for dominance of the mind.

We have seen how some of the greatest philosophers have been driven to the conclusion that imagination is somehow caught up in all our sense-making activities. And as a result, it becomes tied up with our emotions as well. This is a position argued, in the context of education, by Mary Warnock (1976):

> There is a power in the human mind which is at work in our everyday perception of the world, and is also at work in our thoughts about what is absent; which enables us to see the world, whether present or absent as significant. . . . And this power, though it gives us "thought-imbued" perception . . . is not only intellectual. Its impetus comes from the emotions as much as from the reason. (p. 196)

Another sense of imagination that has remained prominent is that most energetically promoted in the Romantic movement. It is the capacity to think of things as possibly being so, our source of novelty, invention, and generativity (White, 1990). "It is imagination which enlarges the bounds of possibility for us, whether for good or ill" (Rousseau, 1911, p. 44).

We have in common a capacity to hold images of what may not be present or even exist in our minds and to allow these images to effect us as though they were present and real. The nature of these images is very hard for us to describe, as they are unlike any other kinds of images we are familiar with in the "external" world. It seems, also, that people might experience these images quite differently—some having clear access to vivid quasi-pictorial images, some having such hazy experiences that the word *image* seems not really the right one. And the same person may be familiar with this range of what seem to be different kinds or degrees of "images." It "is one of those problems where everything is up for grabs, including precisely what the problem is" (Block, 1981, p. 5). Imagination lies at a kind of crux where perception, memory, idea generation, emotion, metaphor, and no doubt other labeled features of our lives intersect and interact. Some of the images we experience seem to be "echoes" of what we have perceived, though we can change them, combine them, manipulate them to become like nothing we have ever perceived. Our memory seems to be able to transform perceptions and store their "echoes" in ways that do not always or perhaps very often require quasi-pictorial "images" (as in the cases of sounds and smells, say). Novelty in ideas has nearly always been connected with the powers of imagination to "see" solutions to problems. Our emotions seem tied to these mental images; when we imagine something we feel as though it is real or present, such that it seems that our "coding" and "access" to images is tied in with our emotions. The logic of imagination seems to conform more readily with that of metaphor than with any scheme of rationality we can be explicit about.

What does this complex set of meanings for imagination suggest about its roles in education?

## IMAGINATION AND EDUCATION

Given these general senses of imagination that we have inherited, we can't escape the fact that it is hardly some trivial feature of our minds. But if it is so important, why has it not been more prominent in educational theory and research? Its troubled history has, on the one hand, made it a suspect, untrustworthy capacity and, on the other, has represented it as somehow in conflict with the rationality that has traditionally been seen as the prime aim of education. On the third hand, of course, is the complexity of the concept. As Herder noted in the 18th century, "Of all the powers of the human mind the imagination has been least explored, probably because it is the most difficult to explore. It seems to be not only the basic and connecting link of all the finer mental powers, but in truth the knot that ties body and mind together" (cited in McFarland, 1985, p. xiii).

The difficulties of doing research on the imagination have ensured that, while implications from research on a range of logical skills and rational capacities have been fed into education, there have been no equivalent implications from research on the imagination. Recognizing the importance of imagination and working out ways to encourage it in students has thus very largely been left to the initiative of individual teachers and parents.

On the fourth hand, it is probably fair to observe that the authorities that determine the curriculum and the social functions of schools have usually dealt ambiguously with the imagination. Such a way of putting it hints at a kind of conspiracy; I don't mean that. Rather, authorities' general recognition that the free play of imagination does not sit easily with order, conventional ideas and systems, neat curriculum schemes, and so on does not encourage them to encourage it. It is treated a little like a visiting rich relation who can be somewhat eccentric and might just run amok at any minute. Even so, Mary Warnock (1976) concluded her examination of the imagination's role in our thinking by claiming that "the cultivation of the imagination . . . should be the chief aim of education" (p. 9).

This is not the general view, of course. Let us try to see why someone might conclude that cultivating the imagination should be central to education by making a kind of inventory of some of its potential uses in our schools. This might help establish why we ought to take imagination more seriously in education. Echoing the preceding gallop through the centuries, I will canter through just a few roles the imagination plays in learning: in resisting conventional, stereotypical thinking; in its relationship with memory and memorizing; in the development of social virtues such as tolerance; in its support of the idea of, and pursuit of, "objective" knowledge; and in its connection with our emotional development.

## Imagination and Conventional Thinking

When we look at typical educational practice, we would be justified in assuming that the main purpose of education is to ensure that students accumulate knowledge, skills, and attitudes appropriate for the lives they are likely to lead. But when we look at the writings of the greatest educational thinkers we find that their main concern is rather different from this. If we consider Plato, Rousseau, and Dewey, for example, it is clear that the accumulation of knowledge and skills in the sense that seems to exercise our schools almost exclusively, is only a small part of what concerns them. What seems to be central to becoming educated, in their view, is not being bound by the conventional ideas and beliefs that people commonly grow up to accept. Education, they passionately assert, is about something that we typically attend to very little in our schools. Instilling knowledge is obviously not irrelevant to them, but their concerns with it are determined by the much more important question of how one enables a student to become an autonomous thinker, able to see conventional ideas for what they are. Education, to put it a bit tendentiously, is a process that awakens individuals to a kind of thought that allows them to imagine conditions other than those that exist or that have existed.

The programs that these great educationalists proposed in order to carry young children to educated adulthood differ. Plato proposed a tightly regimented curriculum taking 50 years to ensure freeing his best students' minds from the constrictions of *doxa*, or conventional opinion. Rousseau proposed manipulating his students' every thought and preventing them from learning to read until about 12 years old, so that they would not be infected by all the secondhand ideas of ordinary social discourse and of books. Dewey proposed methods of instruction designed to encourage students to adopt a scientific, inquiring, and skeptical attitude.

Everyone recognizes that one function of schools is to socialize children, to have them understand, be familiar with, and value the conventional ideas and beliefs of the society of which they are becoming a part. Imagination without such a basis is mere wildness and is unlikely to be fruitful to the individual or to the society. This is a common sentiment: "We want the child not just to be imaginative, but also to be, in some sense, conventional, to learn and to some extent to participate in our shared thoughts, our shared form of life" (Hanson, 1988, p. 137).

Metaphors that are commonly used about educating beyond conventional socializing include "awakening," "freeing," and "releasing." Mental life that is made up very largely of the conventional ideas and opinions of one's time and place is considered a kind of sleep or servitude. (Those who are victims of this sleep or servitude are, of course, unconscious of their condition.) Plato talks of awakening the soul or of freeing prisoners whose experience is of only shadows of reality. Such language constantly recurs in education to catch at that dimension of experience that education is crucially concerned with: "To be able to imagine is to be able to be free of conventional appearances" (Sutton-Smith, 1988, pp. 10–11). Not "must be free" or "free of all conventions all the time," but "able to be free." That is, education is the process that enables us, empowers us, not to be dominated by conventional appearances, ideas, beliefs, and practices. It provides the frame of mind in which we can perceive their utility and accept them as conditions of social life going forward, but in which we can also see their limits and arbitrariness and can imagine changing them should we deem it right to do so.

This means, of course, that there is a constant tension in education between teaching the conventions that students will have to live by and encouraging the capacities that enable them to gain some kind of mental freedom from those conventions—making them tools rather than constraints. This tension is prominent in the writings of the great educational thinkers, but unfortunately is rather less prominent in many schools. The former part of the job, the socializing or inducting students into current conventions, seems to predominate. And this observation is not intended to underestimate how difficult it is to do even this job properly. The power to be free of these conventions tends to be cultivated much less, for many reasons: It is hard; we have no clear curriculum guidelines for achieving it; it clashes with what already takes up so much energy; and, of course, the school's bureaucratic needs for order and various kinds of regimentation exert subtle but powerful pressures against it.

## Imagination in Learning

Since the invention of writing, we have developed elaborate means of storing information. One feature of these systems of storage and recall, whether on wax tablets, on parchment, in books, or in computers, is that what you put in is what you get out. Human learning is in significant ways different from such storage and retrieval. But unfortunately our technologies influence the ways we think about ourselves. Certainly if you learn a fact—say, that water boils at 100 degrees Celsius at sea level—and then repeat that fact later, what you have done looks very similar to what happens if the fact is recorded somewhere in symbols and then later retrieved. It just so happens that in this case the storage device is your brain and the retrieval mechanism is your memory.

If we allow our technologies to determine how we view our intellectual processes, then one effect, which I think has been pervasive and very damaging to education, is to see learning as a process analogous to recording symbols in the mind for later retrieval. The first thing we might note is that the human mind seems to be really very inefficient at this kind of recording and faithful preservation over time. A sheet of paper or a computer disk is much more reliable. Learning in this technology-analogous sense can be measured by how faithfully the records have been preserved by the time they are retrieved during a later test. This kind of testing goes on all the time in schools, and the results are taken very straightforwardly as evidence of learning. This has been going on for so long and so ubiquitously in schools that the meaning of learning that is most common is this kind of mechanical storage and retrieval.

And what's wrong with that? Well, a number of things. Most generally, it ignores what is distinctive about human learning. In particular, it leads to people forgetting that the human mind learns quite unlike the way a computer "learns," and that our memories are quite unlike computer "memories."

The human mind does not simply store facts discretely when it learns. Perhaps it can do this, and we might occasionally use this capacity to remember a phone number or a shopping list in the absence of a piece of paper. More typically when we learn even the simplest fact—that Vasco da Gama set off from Lisbon to sail around in Africa in 1497, arriving in India the following year, or that spiders have eight legs—we do not simply lodge these as discrete data in our brains. As they are learned they mix in with the complex of shifting emotions, memories, intentions, and so on that constitute our mental lives. Facts about spiders will gain an affective coloring connected with our feelings about insects in general and about spiders in particular. Vasco da Gama's voyages may elicit images of ships off alien coasts and evoke a sense of adventure. Whether and how we learn and retain these particular facts is affected by the complex of meaning-structures we already have in place, which in turn are affected by our emotions, intentions, and so on.

The human memory is not an orderly place with slots or shelves for each item, where it remains inert until called for. It is more a shifting turmoil stirred by those emotions and intentions that are a part of us. Virtually nothing emerges from the human memory in the same form in which it was initially learned. All kinds of associations curl around each new fact; there is endless blending and coalescing; and connections are made, broken, and remade. And no small part of this activity involves the imagination.

It is becoming clear that human learning does not involve simply mirroring what is outside the mind, but instead crucially involves constructing or composing (Bruner, 1986). Each mind is different and hass a different perspective on the world. In the process of learning, the student has to fit whatever is to be learned into his or her unique complex of meaning-structures that are already in place. This requires restructuring, composing, and reassessing of meanings. And it is in this ascribing of meaning that Warnock (1976) identifies one of the fundamental activities of imagination.

So taking imagination seriously and then considering learning in light of our developing conception of imagination, we are focusing on those aspects of learning that emphasize meaning. Meaning does not reside in the facts themselves, or in the skills or whatever it is we learn, but in the interaction between what is learned and our minds. And our minds are not simple depositories for facts, but centers of constant activity in which emotions, intentions, and memories all intermingle with what is newly learnt to give it meaning.

This might seem to so hopelessly tangle the casual concept of learning that the simplistic concept that is common in education today seems preferable, despite the educational cost. If we can't teach that a spider has eight legs, for example, without involving emotions, intentions, meaning-structures (whatever they are), and imagination, then we might prefer to throw in the towel. I think the problem is not so bad; we don't somehow have to juggle all these sets of complex mental elements just to talk about learning. Rather, we just have to remember that human learning is something quite different from storing information—and bearing this in mind is not at all difficult. The difficult part, I think, is in taking seriously its implications. And this is where taking imagination seriously begins to play havoc with some of the familiar established elements of the current educational scene.

## Imagination and Memory

In Western culture, from the writings of Aristotle on, there has been a strong connection between memory and imagination. This connection is not merely a historical curiosity; it remains crucially important for education today. There is a tendency, growing out of the rhetoric of progressivism, to consider that rote learning, or learning in the conventional sense discussed above, is educationally useless. The valuable insight in this, about the pointlessness of treating students as though they were storage devices for knowledge that is meaningless to them, has tended to be uncritically generalized to hostility to any kind of memorization. One of the clear implications of the consistent observation of the relationship between memory and imagination is the importance of memorizing knowledge, facts, chunks of prose and poetry, formulas, and so forth for the stimulation and development of the imagination. Ignorance, in short, starves the imagination. And we are ignorant of all that knowledge that we might know how to access, but haven't, or that we have learned how to obtain, but haven't. Only knowledge in our memories is accessible to the action of the imagination.

This principle might seem to run into conflict with that of the previous section. There I seem to be arguing that the imagination is suppressed if students are set to learn lots of knowledge and skills, and here I am claiming that the imagination requires the memorization of lots of knowledge and skills to be adequately stimulated. The two principles are consistent when we observe the point made earlier about the meaningfulness of the knowledge and skills that are to be memorized. Ensuring that knowledge and skills are meaningful requires engaging the imagination in the process of learning. How we can go about ensuring this kind of imaginative learning would require much more space than one chapter provides (see Egan, 1997). What is important to establish here, however, is that the development of students' imaginations will not go forward without their learning and memorizing much and diverse knowledge.

### Social Virtues

I want to add to the list of educational values that follow from the development of the imagination such social virtues as tolerance and justice. Of course it would be too much to say that the evils of the world are caused simply by a lack of imagination, but some of them seem to be so. The lack of that capacity of the imagination that enables us to understand that other people are unique, distinct, and autonomous with lives and hopes and fears quite as real and important as our own is evident in much evil. The development of that imaginative insight does not, however, guarantee that we will then treat them as we wish to be treated ourselves, but it is a necessary prerequisite.

But there are more particular connections to be made between the imagination and social virtues. MacIntyre (1981) argues that the ability to follow stories is connected with the ability to make sense of human experience because our lives are intelligible only within narratives, observing that "man is in his actions and practice, as well as in his fictions, essentially a story-telling animal" (p. 201). It is not merely a mode of entertainment but is complicit in how we make sense of ourselves and how we behave as social animals:

There is no way to give us an understanding of any society, including our own, except through the stock of stories which constitute its initial dramatic resources. Mythology, in its original sense, is at the heart of things. Vico was right and so was Joyce. And so too of course is that moral tradition from heroic stories to its medieval heirs according to which the telling of stories has a key part in educating us into the virtues. (McIntyre, 1981, p. 201)

Stories are good for "educating us into the virtues" because the story not only conveys information and describes events and actions but also engages our emotions. From Plato on, the power of stories to engage, and to engage the commitment of, their hearers has been clear. And it is that power that has made some wary or fearful of them, particularly in educating the young. The powerful stories of the world do not simply describe a range of human qualities; they make us somehow a part of those qualities. They hold up for us, and draw us into, feeling what it would be like to make those qualities a part of ourselves. In this way stories are the tool we have for showing others what it is like to feel as we do and for us to find out what it is like to feel as others do. The story, in short, is "the ability to exchange experiences" (Benjamin, 1969, p. 83). Such stories become, simply, a part of us; as Robert Coles (1989) quotes one of his students: "In a story—oh, like it says in the Bible, the word became flesh" (p. 128).

By imaginatively feeling what it would be like to be other than oneself, one begins to develop a prerequisite for treating others with as much respect as one treats oneself. Prejudice, in the religious, class, or racial forms that we see so commonly, may be seen in part at least as a failure of imaginative development.

The story's power to engage the imagination and contribute thereby to tolerance and a sense of justice needs to be balanced, of course, with its power to do the opposite as well. If the story is one of, say, Aryan superiority and a Nazi salvation, then it can have an equal grasp on the imagination and lead to quite the opposite of toleration and social justice.

What is the protection against this kind of abuse? There seem to me two. The more trivial, recommended by Plato and so many others since, is that we be careful to tell the right kind of stories to children. The more important protection comes from the stimulation of the imagination by a rich and varied stock of stories, as suggested in the previous section. Vulnerability to stories like that of the Nazi's is a result, in part at least, of a mind unfamiliar with, and unsophisticated by, the stock of stories that constitute the culture's resources. The value of familiarity with the stock of stories and the kind of sophistication it brings is that one can understand the fictiveness of stories. The Nazi story is compelling only to people who do not understand fictions and how they work. Not that this is an easy lesson, yielding tidy distinctions between our fictions and reality, but the degree to which we become familiar with the range of stories available in our culture is the degree to which we inoculate ourselves against confusing fiction and reality.

Literature is most commonly assumed to be the part of the curriculum in which we become acquainted with some of the great stories of our culture. Proponents of the educational value of literary studies also commonly argue that they can lead to social virtues. Northrop Frye certainly makes this argument eloquently. After demonstrating various ways in which literature stimulates and develops the imagination, Frye (1963) concludes:

> One of the most obvious uses [of imagination] is its encouragement of tolerance. In the imagination our own beliefs are also only possibilities, but we can also see the possibilities in the beliefs of others. . . . [W]hat produces the tolerance is the power of detachment in the imagination, where things are removed just out of reach of belief and action. (p. 32)

While literature undoubtedly has such a role in encouraging some social virtues, I think we tend to forget that among the great stories of our culture are those expressed in our science, mathematics, history, and so on. Mathematics and science can, if imaginatively taught, build a narrative that provides a context within which the student's life and self become objects to be understood like other objects in the world. The narrative of our science can also contribute importantly to that "detachment in the imagination" that can lead to tolerance and justice.

### Imagination and Objective Knowledge

Imagination is commonly considered quite distinct from whatever mental acts are involved in our attempts to gain objective knowledge. The rich sense of imagination we have inherited, however, seems to lead to the conclusion that quite the opposite is the case. The imagination thus should more properly be seen as one of our major tools in the pursuit of objective knowledge, and indeed as establishing the very conditions of objectivity.

One route to justifying this still-uncommon view may be taken through a point Ruth Mock (1971) makes:

> In the arts and sciences creative imagination demands that an individual frees himself from his immediate preoccupations and associates himself with the medium he is using—the paint, wood, or stone for the painter or sculptor, the words for the writer, the sounds for the musician or the facts for the scientist— so that with it he creates a new form which may to some extent be unexpected even to himself. (p. 21)

What is important for my point here is the observation about the imagination's capacity to inhabit, as it were, the external objects with which it engages. We may see ourselves as distinct beings carving stone, say. But the experienced carver with a well-educated imagination mentally extends into the material being worked, knowing what it is like to break here rather than there, how a stroke here will shear away whatever is below, and so on. That is, the imaginative sculptor—or mathematician or historian—becomes in a curious sense one with the materials he or she is working. That individual feels in high degree something of what Michael Polanyi (1967) has described as a part of "tacit knowledge"—we feel through the tools and objects we work with; they become extensions of our senses and as such are incorporated into our imaginations. And it is not just that the stone, for instance, becomes an extension of ourselves, but that we become an extension of the stone; our minds conform with the nature of the objects that they seek to incorporate, whether those objects are stone and paint, mathematical symbols, historical events, or astrophysical phenomena. The world is not objects out there; insofar as we can know the world, it is within us by means of that curiously reciprocal arrangement whereby we also extend ourselves imaginatively into it.

Well, this is rather airy-fairy language, of course, but it is so because we cannot adequately describe even the simplest functions of our minds with notable clarity, and the more complex can only be pointed at or indicated in such vague terms as those above, in the hope that others will find the pointing and indicating sufficient for them to recognize in their own experience what is meant.

Any area of knowledge, skill, or practice has its own requirements for some form of objectivity; each area has its distinctive rules, structures, forms, and nature, such that our understanding is made up in some significant degree in making our minds conform to them. And while in each area of knowledge, skill, and practice these requirements are different, what is common to them all is their call on the imagination. Objectivity relies on the imaginative capacity to inhabit the forms of the materials, knowledge, skill, or practice one works in.

I think this connection between imagination and objectivity is supported by the connection we commonly make between objectivity and being unprejudiced or being a just judge. We value having someone unprejudiced and objective judge many matters of conflicting interests. Such objectivity draws on the imaginative capacity to see the world from other than the limited perspective of one's own interests. And this is essential not just in relation to the social virtues mentioned earlier; it is a necessary component in adequately understanding any area of knowledge. As such, development of those imaginative capacities that support objectivity is of importance to education.

## Imagination and Emotion

The importance of emotional development to education is no doubt obvious to everyone, and connections between the emotions and imagination are more evident, even in the rather restricted sense of imagination common in educational writing. However superbly skilled or knowledgeable people are, if they lack emotional maturity we recognize them as inadequately educated. Emotional immaturity is a damage that seeps into all aspects of one's life. To suggest that emotional immaturity need not interfere with the development of rationality is to accept, as has been quite common, the desiccated sense of rationality that was so destructive to education during the 20th century. This desiccated sense of rationality has been the focus of most schooling activity, and the belief that reason and emotion were separable parts of us has rendered subservient whatever affects our emotional lives. Taking imagination seriously brings into question the assumptions on which the sidelining of emotions in schooling has been based.

The discourse of education seems to assume that we have an intellectual part of us and an emotional part of us, or a cognitive and affective part, and that these can sensibly be separated. It has become at least operationally the case that schooling is responsible primarily for the cognitive or intellectual part. One can, of course, try to ignore the affective dimensions of, say, mathematics and treat that area of human experience as a purely cognitive set of procedures to be learned. What is achieved by so doing is at best to make mathematics something of merely utilitarian value and to destroy its other potential values to our lives. The great wonder and fun of mathematics as a human activity that has enchanted many is largely destroyed in schooling for nearly everybody, including those who are "good at it," when it is taught in the typical desiccated way. Some lucky few can discover the pleasures of mathematics as adults, but for most it is useful only when making change or keeping accounts.

The wasteland called school mathematics is perhaps the most obvious casualty of the attempt to separate something deemed rational, cognitive, intellectual from imagination and emotion. The result is a disaster because it is built on false assumptions about human learners. The task we face is not simply to point out that mathematics is a passionate affair that can become engaging and meaningful only when students' imaginations make contact with the passion within it. The problem is that the very language of educational discourse is so infected with assumptions and presuppositions that need to be uprooted and challenged that people have great difficulty grasping how mathematics could be different from the way it presently is. For most people mathematics is what is in the textbooks. How we might reinject imagination and emotion into such a mathematics generates a blank, because the textbooks presuppose that imagination and emotion are largely irrelevant to mathematics. This belief persists despite the very plain passion and imaginative genius of those people who generated the mathematical knowledge that is embalmed in textbooks.

The separation of emotion and intellect, I have argued already, has been educationally dysfunctional. We need to recapture Wordsworth's sense of imagination as "Reason in her most exhalted mood" (1805/1991, 14, 192) and see the force of Frye's (1963) observation that "the combination of emotion and intellect [is what] we call imagination" (p. 57). Taking imagination seriously in education directs us to transcend the intellect/ emotion split and perceive both together in all areas of knowledge and all aspects of education. Our emotional lives are tied to our imaginations and our imaginations are tied to our intellects. Imaginative learning, then, inevitably involves our emotions. Imagination is important to education because it compels us to recognize that forms of teaching and learning that are disconnected from our emotions are educationally barren.

Now, none of this is to suggest that typical classrooms are in future to be aflood with tears, wailing, and wild joy all day long. Rather, I propose that whatever content is to be dealt with needs to be attached to students' emotions in some way, or that the human emotions that generated the content in the first place, or that attach to it in whatever way, need to be a part of what is dealt with in the class. (Elsewhere I have tried to show how this can be routinely achieved; for example, see Egan, 1997).

## CONCLUSION

I have included a wide range of features in this attempt to sketch reasons why imagination is important to education. Perhaps some of you might feel that I have included too much and that the result is a sense of imagination being involved in everything of educational importance. Such a reading would not mistake my intention, but I would want to argue that this sense would not include too much. Indeed, I think imagination should properly be very pervasive in education. Such a view is difficult to take only if we think of imagination as a thing, as a particular, distinct part of the mind. If we see it, instead, as a particular kind of flexibility, energy, and vividness that can imbue all mental functions, as a kind of mood of mind, then its role in the topics I have mentioned becomes easier to understand. To be imaginative, then, is not to have a particular function highly developed, but to have heightened capacity in all mental functions. It is not, in particular, something distinct from reason, but rather is what gives reason flexibility, energy, and vividness. It makes all mental life more meaningful; it makes life more abundant. Dewey (1966) expressed this sense of the pervasiveness of imagination thus: "Imagination is as much a normal and integral part of human activity as is muscular movement" (p. 237).

An association of our current rich conception of imagination with Romanticism and romance perhaps merits a final brief note. One of the central romantic images is of the heroic journey as an allegory of our lives. It might be useful to let this image color our sense of a more imaginative kind of education than is commonly provided today. The process of education would thus be seen, quite properly, as a heroic journey, full of wonders, mysteries, dangers, obstacles, and so on. While schooling today might not readily evoke such an image, education as a heroic journey gives us a sense of the direction in which we might try to move schools. And those who would like to make schooling more like an imaginative and heroic journey for students may take heart in seeing their own present struggles as also a heroic journey, through the tangles of debased educational language and the obstacles of institutionalized commitments to narrow conformity and utility, in the direction of something more wonderful.

*Chapter 2*

# Imagination in the Context of Modern Educational Thought

## KEIICHI TAKAYA

In this chapter I shall argue that the development of the person's imagination[1] must be a crucial part of education. This argument is, of course, based on a particular view of imagination and of education. My observation is that, while the development of imagination must logically be a necessary part of achieving the educational goals that we inherit from the educational ideas of the modern West, this connection is not particularly made explicit or appreciated in educational principle and practice today except by a few educational theorists. One of the major reasons seems to me a conceptual confusion, and therefore, I will try to make it clear. I certainly do not intend to say that the legacy of Western educational thought should be accepted in its entirety, or that it is necessarily superior to other traditions, but I suggest that some central values are worth supporting and the development of imagination constitutes a crucial part of this project.

Although the development of imagination is not a direct function of intention and control (not a product simply of instructional input, personal effort, or amount of information), it is not totally outside our control (not simply a matter of divine gift, genius, or natural unfolding), either. For the development of imagination to be a justifiable educational concern, it must be shown, first, that imagination is a worthy and necessary part of educational values and, second, that it is possible for instructional processes and activities to influence its development. My response to both these claims is affirmative. First, I think that such educational values as understanding with breadth and depth, rationality, and morality by definition require imaginative capacity. Second, one cannot become imaginative without knowledge or skill, which are acquired through experience that include instructional processes.

The idea of imagination started to become prominent in general philosophy and literary theory by the 17th century, particularly by philosophers who thought and wrote in response to John Locke (e.g., Gottfried Wilhelm Leibniz,

Étienne Bonnot de Condillac, and David Hume). Through the influence of German idealism (e.g., Johannes N. Tetens, Immanuel Kant, and Friedrich Schiller), it became a central value and a major epistemological concept of romanticism (e.g., William Wordsworth and Samuel T. Coleridge). Although it was empiricism that attracted most followers, the educationists whose ideas and practices affected the formation of our education today had strong theoretical roots in romanticism and idealism (e.g., Johann H. Pestalozzi, Johann F. Herbart, Friedrich W. Froebel). However, even when the ideas that have romantic and idealistic roots became influential, the quintessential romantic idea, imagination, was not considered relevant. It was regarded, at worst, as contradictory and a hindrance to the development of reason (e.g., it inflates unnecessary and unrealistic desire) and, at best, desirable but not essential (e.g., recreation, help in memorization, useful device for rhetoric), even by those thinkers who were strongly influenced by romantic ideas. It was not until the 20th century that pragmatists regarded imagination as part of rationality and some psychologists began to overcome reductionistic psychology (classical empiricism, behaviorism, and Herbart's psychology of presentations). Vygotsky's interest in higher mental functions, for example, came to locate imagination as one of the major educational values.

## THE CONNECTION BETWEEN
## IMAGINATIVENESS AND EDUCATEDNESS

The purposes of this section are, first, to present my basic thesis that an educated person must be, at least to some extent, an imaginative person and, second, to show that, while there are various ideas on what imagination means, modern Western culture has a certain preference for a certain kind of imagination.

Richard Kearney (1994) argues that when talking about imagination we should avoid both extreme essentialism and extreme nominalism (p. 16). The former implies that there is an identifiable core or timeless essence of what imagination means. This position is typically and historically called the *faculty conception* of the imagination, and it is based on philosophical assumptions that have been challenged for the past 100 years or so. The latter implies that imagination means anything we like to call by that name, and it leads to an extreme form of relativism. Although various writers have mentioned imagination (or equivalent terms[2]) and various definitions, meanings, implications, and emotional tones have been attached to the idea, the notion of imagination is not totally random, as an extreme nominalist position may suggest. There is a certain level of agreement on what it means and why it is important, and I understand that most of the shared meanings and implications are strongly connected to what we today regard as educational values to be pursued.

## DEFINING IMAGINATION

I define imagination, following Kieran Egan (1992a), as a flexibility of the mind (p. 36). By *flexibility*, I mean that a person has the ability and tendency to think of things in a way that is not tightly constrained by the actual, such as conventions, cultural norms, one's habitual thought, and information given by others. In conceptualizing imagination, I draw on two theorists (Kieran Egan and Robin Barrow), but I also want to stress that, though I borrow particular words and expressions from the two individuals, the ideas themselves are widely shared among the theorists of imagination today (and to some extent by historical figures too).

First, I want to distinguish imagination from two similar terms: *creativity* and *critical thinking*. Essentially, I think that the distinction is a matter of context. Creativity implies imaginativeness in the context of production of objects and ideas, for example, aesthetic creativity and problem solving (cf. Egan and Nadaner, 1988, p. xi); critical thinking implies imaginativeness in the context of sense-making or understanding, for example, social and moral understanding and literary criticism. These distinctions are, however, not rigid.

### Kieran Egan and the "Flexibility of the Mind"

Kieran Egan (1992) claims, "Imaginativeness is not a well-developed, distinct function of the mind, but is rather a particular flexibility which can invigorate all mental functions" (p. 36).[3] By taking up the way Egan conceptualizes imagination, I want, first, to point out certain reasons why imagination has attracted some educational theorists and, second, to get rid of some misleading philosophical assumptions and language that have been historically attached to the concept of imagination.

First, and above all, one of the major attractions of the idea of imagination is to emphasize the distinctive nature of human cognition (learning, thinking, etc.), and Egan is probably the strongest advocate of this aspect. The idea of imagination has always symbolized freedom of human thoughts; epistemologically, it symbolizes the active nature of the mind, as opposed to the view that regards the mind as passive and mechanical, such as the Enlightenment empiricists and sensationists (e.g., Locke, Condillac, and Helvetius), the behavioristic view of the human mind (a view that reduces the functions of the human mind to the relation between stimulus and response), and the practical application of the behavioristic principle (i.e., overemphasis on rote memorization; it regards the human mind as something like a floppy disk).

One of the important beliefs of the modern era is that of the educability or perfectibility of human beings. Recalling Locke's tabula rasa or Helvetius's belief in the omnipotence of education, modern educational theorists tried to show that individuals, separated from particular community or class, can acquire, by education, what they essentially need in their lives as human beings and that these individuals can be made into individuals who can contribute to the construction of a new society free of prejudice resulting from particular social or cultural traditions. However, the other side of the coin was the conception of the human mind as passive, which overemphasizes manipulability from the environment. As a reaction to this view, particularly in the Romantic movement, a new conception of the human mind was born, and the idea of imagination was the most characteristic idea. In this period of time, as Abrams (1953) argues, the metaphor of the human mind changed from "mirror" to "lamp," that is, from a mechanism that merely receives and reflects what is given from without to an organism that projects as well as receives. Or, as McFarland (1985) says, while the idea of the soul as the divine element (i.e., creative faculty) in human nature rapidly lost its explanatory force as a corollary to the decline of religion and theology (as part of the Enlightenment rejection of arbitrary authority), the idea of imagination took up the epistemological explanation of creative capacity. In educational theories, this shift in the view of the human mind manifested itself as an emphasis on children's curiosity and interest, their distinctive modes of learning, and the belief that mere presentation of objects is not enough to secure educational results.

However, for a long time the idea of imagination, though appreciated in general philosophy and literary theory, was not seen as relevant to the new perspectives in education. Throughout the 19th century, when many influential educational ideas were formulated, educational thinkers continued to see imagination as, first, a faculty of manipulating images and, second, a hindrance to reason for its rootedness in bodily senses and desire.[4]

Second, there is some misleading language to be eliminated, and Egan's definition is the result of doing so. They are the "faculty" conception of the imagination, an almost exclusive connection between imagining and imaging (visualization), and the confusion between imaginative and imaginary.

## The Faculty Conception

Traditionally, imagination has been regarded as a "faculty" (or "power") of the mind that generates images ("mental pictures") by associating and dissociating "ideas" and "impressions." However, as a result of 20th-century philosophy and psychology, the faculty conception and the kind of language that tend to go with it are now avoided except as a metaphorical explanation.

The faculty conception implies that it is possible to identify a special means to develop the imagination per se just as there is a way to develop a specific muscle, because the term *faculty* or *power* implies that there is something specific (a specifiable part of the mind or brain) that we can work on and influence. However, imaginative capacity seems unlike that.

## Imagination, Imagining, and Imaging

It is usually said that there are two kinds of imagination: reproductive and productive (creative). The former is an ability to separate and combine various images or perceptual data so that the whole makes some sense. The underlying assumption is that these data come through the senses to the mind in the form of atomistic elements (e.g., Locke's "simple ideas"). The productive imagination performs similar operations but creates new images that do not exist in reality or have not been thought of before. These classifications have been around for a few centuries at least. Some of the philosophical assumptions underlying them have been challenged, particularly in 20th-century philosophy and psychology (e.g., phenomenology and analytic philosophy) and are now largely discarded.

For example, the epistemological assumption of the rigid separation between perception and thought, which underlies many modern philosophers' theory of imagination, is not accepted today. Arnheim (1969) contends that "the cognitive operations called thinking are not a privilege of mental processes above and beyond perception but the essential ingredients of perception itself" (p. 13). He gives the following example:

> A box, partly covered by a flowerpot, is seen as a complete cube partly hidden. This means that perceptual organization does not limit itself to the material directly given but enlists invisible extensions as genuine parts of the visible. (p. 34)

Some of the old epistemological languages are no longer taken literally; they are used as either metaphorical explanations of our process of thought or terms to describe analytic distinctions (as opposed to ontological distinctions).

The connection between imagining and imaging does not seem to be as tight as formerly believed to be. Educational theorists in the early 20th century and some psychologically oriented theorists (e.g., McMillan, Kirkpatrick) tend either to largely identify imagining with imaging (visualizing), or to focus on imaging (visualizing) as the most important aspect of imagining. However, more recent thinkers (e.g., Warnock, White, Egan, Greene), particularly those who are familiar with analytic philosophy, are very clear about the distinction and tend to give imagining different significance. For example, White (1990) writes, "The imagery of a sailor scrambling ashore could be exactly the same as that of his twin brother crawling backwards into the sea, yet to imagine one of these is quite different from imagining the other" (p. 92). So, he says, "imagination does not imply imagery since much imagination is of what is non-sensory" (p. 88). It is better for us not to associate imagining exclusively with imaging or imagery. As Egan vis-à-vis White suggests, being imaginative implies more than being able to have vivid and various mental pictures; an imaginative person is one who can think, feel, and perceive with a large degree of flexibility.[5]

*Imaginative and Imaginary*

Among educational theorists of imagination today, there seems to be a certain preference for the kind of imaginative capacity that is worth pursuing. For example, the kind of imagination we appreciate is different from mere dreaming or fantasizing as a way of wish fulfillment. Rather, imagination is discussed as a means to become aware of the actual world more accurately, or as a necessary part of being critical of actual society (e.g., Warnock, Egan, Greene, McCleary, Johnson).

## Robin Barrow and the Criterion of "Unusual and Effective"

The second theorist I draw on is Robin Barrow (1988, 1990). Barrow (1988) defines imagination as follows: "The criteria of imagination are, I suggest, unusualness and effectiveness. To be imaginative is to have the inclination and ability consciously to conceive of the unusual and effective in particular contexts" (p. 84).[6]

By taking up Barrow's argument, I want, first, to get rid of the assumption that there is a generic capacity called imagination that can be used across domains; second, to emphasize that the criteria of imaginativeness include consciousness, intention, or will; and third, to suggest that there is a certain preference in our culture for various conceptions of imagination. The third issue implies that the value of imagination is relative to other educational values: imagination is not valuable on its own.

It is hard to sustain an argument that there is a nonspecific, general power called imagination. It is hard to think that there are persons who are generally imaginative, except when we emphasize the attitudinal aspect of imaginativeness (see sections below). This is so because all forms of thought including imagination (also, for example, "critical thinking") need contents of thought, and contents usually means knowledge and skill that are to a large extent specific to the field of research or activities.

According to Barrow, imaginative ideas and acts are not merely the ones that are peculiar. They must also be excellent and effective in light of standards in the respective field. (Of course, there are cases in which we call someone "imaginative" ironically.) An imaginative soccer player, an imaginative painter, and an imaginative teacher are not called so just for the sake of unusualness. A person who is imaginative in one area of activity may or may not be so in different areas of activity (an imaginative painter may or may not be an imaginative teacher of art).

When we apply the term *imaginative* to a product or to an idea, we imply that they are the result of an intention to produce that effect even if some accidental elements are involved. Something that merely happens to be so is not usually called imaginative. Although linguistic or conceptual analysis may not show much other than the linguistic habit of those who use the language, this interpretation of the term *imaginative* seems relevant, because, for example, if we eliminate this criterion of intention, the issue of imaginativeness becomes simply a matter of divine inspiration or luck, which is beyond instruction.

If Barrow's argument about the context specificity of the imagination is acceptable, it should also be accepted that there is a problem about what kind(s) of imagination (i.e., imagination in what context) should be valued. (The idea of context, i.e., areas of activity, however, may need to be revised. The "areas" are not as clearly demarcated as it used to be supposed by theorists such as Paul Hirst [1969].) One widely shared concern is moral imagination, and it tends to be discussed in relation to such concepts as empathy and care (cf. Greene, 1995; Johnson, 1993). I am not depreciating imagination in other areas, say, music; but I want to suggest that, first, in education, particularly in terms of schooling, the development of imaginative capacity in certain areas seems to matter more than in others, and second, indeed there seem to be certain preferred areas among contemporary theorists of imagination.

## Imagination as a Combination of Several Factors

I think that imaginativeness is a combination of several factors rather than a result of a single power of the mind, and that a person is imaginative in some area(s) and not in general. For people to be imaginative, they need knowledge, skill, curiosity, and other factors that may be innate or acquired, conscious or unconscious, though the entire list of these factors has not been, and probably will never be, identified. There are various conditions of imaginativeness discussed by various theorists, for example, knowledge, unconscious (or nonconscious), emotional engagement, and so forth. There is no definitive answer to these issues, and I certainly do not intend to give one (because I cannot). I present what I think imagination means and the possibilities and conditions of developing the imagination through instructional activities and processes.

However, one concession should be made. It is what may be called an attitudinal aspect of imaginativeness, and I may describe it as a playful attitude, a fondness of experimenting with various ideas. In describing the criteria of imaginativeness, Barrow says that the imaginative person has the *inclination* as well as the ability to be both unusual and effective (Egan & Nadaner, 1988). The term *inclination* may be interpreted to mean the frequency of producing some products (ideas or objects) that are both unusual and effective, but I think that it implies something of the person's favorable attitude toward entertaining a variety of ideas and perspectives. This aspect of imaginativeness may not be specific to the context or content, and it may also to some extent be transferable from one area to another.

## AN EDUCATED PERSON MUST BE AN IMAGINATIVE PERSON

Education is a process of socialization, acculturation, or conventionalization, since it is almost impossible to consider a person "educated" if he or she is devoid of knowledge, conventions, and so forth that characterize a given society or a culture. The purpose of education may also include the development of the capacity to distance oneself to a certain extent from the values and patterns of thought of a particular society (for example, morality, which is an important part of education, means more than following cultural conventions or societal rules), but it certainly is not to produce misfits who are not aware of what is going on around them.

Considering these, I want to suggest that there are at least three ways in which an educated person must be imaginative. (I want to stress that these criteria of educatedness are not completely arbitrary; they are based on reasonably shared views on educational values.) What people mean by being "educated" varies according to such conditions as cultural background and personal preference, but I think that the following aspects of educatedness are, first, shared reasonably widely, and, second, worth supporting; and they have imaginativeness as a crucial feature.

First, educational philosophers since ancient times have spoken of the distinction between being merely knowledgeable and being educated. From this perspective, I want to suggest that educated persons must be able to understand the meaning or significance of what they experience or know by placing it in a larger context that may not be given in the immediate facts, information, or data. This implies that educated persons must have a sense that there is something beyond what is immediately given. This sense may very well lead to, or require, a sense that there are alternative possibilities to what they have here and now.

Second, overlapping to some extent with the first characteristics of educatedness, and as is seen in such phrases as *lifelong learning, learning how to learn*, or *education as growth*, educated persons must have an ability and willingness to pursue further education. Being able and willing to pursue further education logically means that they can see alternative possibilities, that is, possibilities that they may be mistaken, that there are other ways of interpreting the facts and events, or that there is more to see in the world. Warnock (1976), for instance, writes about what education can give, saying that education gives the sense "that there is always *more* to experience, and *more in* what we experience than we can predict" and does not let people "[succumb] to a feeling of futility, or to the belief that they have come to an end of what is worth having" (pp. 202–3; italics in original).

Third, educated persons must be moral persons in terms of, at least, moral understanding. Morality involves various factors. In order to be moral, people need to have knowledge, affection, will, and so on, for which, I think, imaginativeness is crucial. For example, an ethic of care, which is widely discussed as a theory of morality and moral education, says that care is not complete unless it is received by the one cared for.[7] This implies, I think, that for us to care about other people, we need to work out what is good for the ones we care about, for which mere sentiment is not enough.[8] This requires the ones who care to step out of their own values and perspectives and try to understand those of the ones about whom they care. Thus, moral persons must be able to go beyond their own perception, thoughts, and feelings and see things from other people's point of view.

The third criterion, morality, may not be included in the criteria of educatedness from an analytic point of view based on the common usage of the term *educated* in English. However, there are some strands of educational theories both in the past and present which give as much emphasis to morality as to such things as academic adequacy. First, in the history of education, moral education has always been a major concern of education (e.g., education as *Bildung*), and it may be arguable that the priority given to useful skills and knowledge (as is seen in our society from Herbert Spencer's appreciation of science for utilitarian reason to the "back to basics" movement) may be an exception rather than a norm. Second, I appreciate the criticisms against the primacy of a particular type of academic adequacy over other values, notably by Nel Noddings's ethic of care, and want to suggest that morality should be included in the criteria of educatedness.

Thus, I observe that the widely shared conception of educatedness by definition implies the necessity of imaginativeness, and I propose that we keep the three criteria, whatever else may be added, as minimum criteria of educatedness. The imagination as a capacity to transcend actuality is a crucial factor in all of them.

## THE RELATIONS BETWEEN
## EDUCATION, SCHOOLING, AND IMAGINATION

### Imaginative Development and Education

I believe that while instructional processes or activities that do not develop the imagination are a failure, imagination apart from other educational values is not of much worth. There may be cases where a person is highly imaginative in a certain area (let's say, playing chess) but he or she is terrible in other respects. In such a case, imaginativeness does not seem to be particularly valuable in light of the person's overall education.

Educational values are determined, to a large extent, by social, cultural, and historical contingencies, and the reason why imagination is valued or what sort of imagination is valued is also partly determined by our particular social contingencies. The idea of imagination as an epitome of human freedom reflects our hope to transcend these limitations (cf. Greene, 1995, pp. 51, 163), but we have, whether we like it or not, certain preferences about the kinds of imagination that have close connection with our cultural values. It is in the context of schooling where this issue becomes explicit, because school is the place where cultural and social values are presented, both explicitly and implicitly, to individual children, while education, though depending on how it is defined, can be more personal.

I am aware that the way I conceptualize the imagination may sound very much like Rousseau's (1762/1979) conception of reason when he says, "Of all the faculties of man, reason, which is, so to speak, only a composite of all the others, is the one that develops with the most difficulty and latest" (p. 89). I may be interpreted as saying that children do not have imagination. Not exactly so. What I want to suggest is similar to Chambliss's (1974) understanding of Rousseau's view of reason in childhood. Chambliss argues that Rousseau is not saying that children do not have reason, but that children are yet to develop a particular sort of reason (p. 52). I would apply this logic to imagination. Although children have imaginative capacity, it is not to be regarded as the kind of imaginative capacity that educational theorists tend to appreciate in relation to other educational values such as reflective capacity and empathy.

That being said, there are two issues I want to discuss. First, the imagination as flexibility of the mind may exhibit itself as fantasy or play, and these phenomena are more abundant in childhood. This sort of imagination may be valuable and charming, but it is not by itself the kind of imaginativeness that is seen in such educational values as broader understanding and morality. Treasuring and keeping alive children's imagination, as such theorists as Cobb (1977) and Singer and Singer (1990) suggest, may be a key to the imagination in a highly developed sense. However, the connection between these must be examined in order not to fall into unfruitful and simplistic rhetoric or to end up with mere slogans.

Second, overall, the kind of imagination we value has a strong connection with rationality, not in the positivist's sense of scientific thinking or in the classical sense of reason as an intuitive faculty to grasp the universal truths. The reason I have in mind is more akin to pragmatism's notion of reflective capacity. For example, Peirce (1896–1899/1955) writes, "When a man desires ardently to know the truth, his first effort will be to imagine what that truth can be" (p. 43), which is a hypothetical thinking in scientific thought. Or, as Dewey (1916/1985) says, imagination is what "makes any activity more than mechanical" (p. 244), which is similar to the notion of imagination as flexibility of the mind. Coupled with the importance of verification of one's ideas against factual evidence, pragmatists regard imaginative aspects of thought as a necessary part of good thinking, and this inclusion of imaginative capacity as part of rationality is relatively new.

Today, by and large, imagination is seen as a part of healthier or more balanced rationality. There may be other ways of conceptualizing imagination, but I believe that the imagination as conceptualized as such is a crucial part of educational values. There are, then, a few kinds of arguments or rhetoric to be avoided.

## Kinds of Rhetoric to Be Avoided

The first is a view that sees education and imagination as antithetical. The second is the view that sees education and imagination as irrelevant to each other. These views are typically seen in the overly romantic view of imagination and childhood and tend to suggest that imagination is at its peak or in its ideal form in childhood and will be lost as children grow.

Education, or more accurately, the instructional process, is sometimes talked about as if it were antithetical to imagination. This is typically seen in the positions and arguments that overromanticize certain types of imaginative and creative activities of children or of artists. One of the earliest examples of this view (though it is not my intention to suggest that he is responsible for such an overromanticized view) can be seen in Wordsworth (1807), when he praises a child by calling him "Thou best Philosopher" and sings, "Heavens lies about us in our infancy! / Shades of the prison-house begin to close / Upon the growing Boy." An example of this belief applied to educational theory is Lev N. Tolstoi, who thought that artistic creativity would develop only if materials and stimuli for creation were given to children and said that children were closer than adults to the ideal of truth and beauty.

In many—probably all—domains of experience, it is impossible to exhibit one's imaginativeness without having requisite skills and knowledge in the field. Soccer players cannot move imaginatively unless they know certain rules and standard tactics and are capable of certain movements. In many areas in which we tend to think that imaginativeness is crucially important, things that can be acquired through education and experience are necessary. For example, being imaginative about a social issue, say, as a part of empathizing with the fate of refugees in a foreign country, means next to nothing unless we are able to think of what their situation is really like or what they really need. This requires lots of information and understanding (history, politics, economy, nutrition, and psychology), because otherwise, we will end up projecting our own values, which tend to be widely off the mark of the real needs of the people in the tragic situation.

Moreover, there is a danger in the logic and rhetoric of regarding the development of imagination as a matter of releasing children's inborn potentials. Diggins's account of Dewey's growing disenchantment with child-centered practice expresses this concern nicely:

> To allow the student to follow his own "desires" is to assume that learning springs mysteriously "from uncontrolled haphazard sources." In truth there is no spontaneous germination in mental life. If he does not get the suggestion from the teacher, he gets it from somebody or something in the home or the street or from what some more vigorous fellow pupil is doing. (Dewey, quoted in Diggins, 1994, p. 312)

This is not to say that school or systematic teaching is always right or a guarantee to imaginative development. But it seems to suggest that the development of imaginative capacity as part of rationality needs education in terms of systematic instructional processes and activities.

Education and imagination are also talked about as if they were irrelevant to each other. Education tends to be considered incapable of making people more imaginative. Similarly, imagination tends to be considered incapable of contributing to making people more educated. The former problem seems to be rooted in the conception of imagination as a single, innate, or transcendental capacity: imagination as a "power" of the mind that is separate from such educable factors as knowledge and skills. The latter problem seems to be mainly from the traditional association of imaginative activities with artistic activities—a view that sees imagination as mostly concerned with art, and art as a frill in education.

These kinds of misguided arguments are not so common in academic writings, but very common in less formal discussions and arguments. On the surface, the idea of developing the imaginative capacity through art is shared by many theorists, for example, by Dewey, Steiner, McMillan, Cobb, Swanger, Johnson, and Greene, but they do not simply say that encouraging children's artistic activities in terms of free expression would guarantee the development of imagination, and they are aware of the distinctive nature and limitations of art. Compared with their views, the following argument is simplistic. In an article titled "Art Education Means Business," Carol Sterling (1994) writes:

> Art education builds the skills businesses need in their employees. The world of work has changed dramatically in the last two decades. Routinized behavior is out, and the ability to adapt, diagnose problems, and find creative solutions—even at the most basic levels of production and service delivery—is now crucial. (p. 37)

She then notes that the "skills" that businesses need these days, and art education can build, are "how to imagine and how to apply [the] imaginations to real business problems." This argument seems to overlook the distinction between art and business, and also is not explicit or clear about what imagination means.

Another example is found in an article by Brenda Casey (n.d.). Although she acknowledges that "imagination is not something that children are born with" (and hence needs education), she associates imagination too closely with play: "Very young children are fascinated by their fingers and toes. Old favourites like 'Two Little Dicky Birds', 'Round and Round the Garden', and 'This Little Piggy' are guaranteed ways of engaging the imagination." She concludes by saying, "Remember, the child whose imagination is fulfilled will grow to be resourceful and creative adult." I do not think that the development of creativity (whatever she means by it) is "guaranteed" by "fulfilling" the child's imagination (as she conceives it).

These problems can be, and need to be, overcome by clarifying what we mean by imagination, what elements constitute imagination, and how education can contribute to the development of these elements. Since imaginativeness is not a result of a single faculty that we are born with, it is at least to some extent, educable; however, we cannot just train it in, say, art and expect that it could be transferred to other domains.

Therefore, I think that education, to a larger extent than is usually recognized, has a very important role to play in making people imaginative, and imagination in making people educated.

I do not think that the romanticized view of imagination and childhood is without reason or pointless, because it is true that there are some cases in which education (particularly schooling) imposes a certain pattern of thought or a certain value system. It is commonly observed that children lose enthusiasm about learning or what seems to be a flexible, lively way of thinking and feeling as they grow up. It may be valid to praise the children's "imagination" or "creativity" as an antithesis to society's tendency to mold children's thought to a certain pattern. However, imagination or creativity in such a sense is not by itself worthwhile unless it is made part of other intellectual, moral, and aesthetic traits. The task for educators is, then, first, to make clear the connection between children's imaginative tendencies and educated imaginativeness and, second, if there is such a connection, to figure out ways to keep what seems to be an imaginative tendency of the children while connecting it to other educational values.

Here again, we have to be cautious about the meaning or implication that we attach to the term *imaginative*. For example, while some people think that many of the artworks made by children simply lack skill, others praise them, regarding them as products of children's imagination. I am not suggesting that we should not praise children's artworks in any sense. I think that children's paintings or poems might be described as imaginative, but we need to be cautious here. The judgment that children's works of art are imaginative—usually a judgment that they are different from adults' conventional works—is possible only from the adult's point of view; it is a judgment possible only for adults who have seen many works of art and are familiar with (and probably tired of) conventions. Children are likely to be merely using whatever perspective, skills, or vocabulary are available to them and are not necessarily conscious of their unusualness. (It may be a contentious issue whether to include the clause "being aware of one's own unusualness" in the definition of imaginativeness. Barrow is clearly including this in his definition of imagination, but others may disagree.) As Barrow suggests, unusualness or peculiarity alone does not constitute imaginativeness.

Thus I propose to distinguish two uses of the expression imaginative. One is what I may call an objective sense, which is close to Barrow's use: When we call, for example, a scientist, an athlete, or a teacher imaginative, we are suggesting that the person exhibits both unusualness and effectiveness in his or her performance in the respective field. This sense of imaginativeness is concerned mainly with objective evaluation of the quality of an idea or a performance.

The other is what we might call an educational sense; when we call a child imaginative, we are not always concerned with the objective excellence of his or her achievement. Rather, when calling a child, or what he or she does, "imaginative," we are likely to be suggesting the fact that the child seems to be surpassing what he or she has already achieved. The child may not be doing anything unusual or effective in light of objective standards, but still, what the child is doing may be regarded as surpassing what he or she has achieved so far (thus, "unusual and effective" for him- or herself). Or we are praising the child's enthusiasm, lively curiosity, or passion for the subject because it seems to suggest that the child would develop a sustained engagement with the subject, and possibly produce a really imaginative product someday. The imaginativeness in this sense may not mean much to people other than the child's parents or caretaker, or unless we have a good reason to believe that the child's imaginative tendency will lead him or her toward significant imaginative achievements. The significance is, in short, educational (or "formative" as opposed to "summative," borrowing Michael Scriven's terms [Eisner, 1985, pp. 173, 198]). As Jerome Bruner says, first-rate scientists working at the frontier of their fields and children working at their own frontier have at least this in common; they are trying to surpass what they have achieved so far (1960/1977, p. 14; 1962, p. 126). And this attempt to go beyond what they have achieved so far is a crucial factor that leads to intellectual, aesthetic, and moral development. In this sense, what appears to be trivial may be educationally meaningful to the children themselves and to those who are concerned with their education.

Although contemporary theorists of imagination define imagination as a capacity to be flexible in thought (and I certainly agree with them), there are some suggestions that imagination does not exactly fit the definition as a capacity; they suggest that imagination includes something more or that it has something different. For example, Dewey (1987) says that imagination "designates a quality that animates and pervades all processes of making and observation" (p. 271); Bailin (1994) includes "free play" and "exploration" as well as "the generation of ideas" in her idea of imagination (p. 121); Singer and Singer (1990) think that imagination, distinct from creativity, "is fun in its own right whether or not it contributes to a public product"(p. 270) and is "a playful, creative spirit" (p. 268). These aspects may be close to something like spirit or attitude; it may not make sense from the perspective of conceptual analysis, but I do not think it is wise to simply dismiss it.

It is common to say that children are, in some respects, more imaginative than adults. There are some problems with this notion, but it seems to contain a degree of truth. To be imaginative, we need a certain perception of what the actuality is. So it may be justified to say that children are less imaginative because they do not have experience or knowledge by which to perceive the actual. However, we know that children tend to have a much more lively curiosity than adults, or a strong tendency to strive to go beyond what they have already acquired. Moreover, they are much less conventionalized than adults. So it may also be justified to say that children are generally more imaginative than adults. The point is that we have to be careful about the context in which we apply the term.

Further, somewhat contrary to Bruner's view, mentioned above, there are arguments that regard children's way of thinking and feeling as fundamentally different from adults'. One example is found in Egan (2002). He says that there are "trade-offs" as a person grows (p. 92) and that the process of growth or education is not simply a matter of one-directional progress or accumulation. There may be something that people lose as they grow up. This is certainly not an isolated view, and though I think that the kind of imaginativeness we tend to pursue requires instructional processes, there may be cases in which the very instructional processes restrict the development of imagination. For example, McMillan (1904/1923) makes a good point when she says that the grasp of new vision, which I understand to be what we mean by the grasp of alternative possibilities or new ideas, is not caused by experience and observation, even though they may help (pp. 140–141). If imaginativeness develops cumulatively because of instructional processes, imaginative capacity is supposed to increase as an individual has more experience and observation. However, this is not the case. So it seems reasonable to gather that there may be something like "trade-offs." An example of the trade-off kind of view is Edith Cobb's (1977/1993) argument that highly creative persons tend to attribute their creativity to their experience of a certain type of sensation that they felt in childhood. Cobb's argument is based on her research into biographical and autobiographical materials of highly imaginative/creative people around the world. Although it is not exactly a scientifically testable claim, I think that it still deserves to be taken into account, because such empirical observations may very well show what conceptual analysis cannot show.

## IMAGINATION AND MODERN WESTERN EDUCATION

Education as we know it today (particularly as it has been developed in the modern West) is founded on an assumption about what we should expect from our lives. It is a belief that "becom[ing] increasingly mindful with regard to [one's] lived situation—and its untapped possibilities" (Greene, 1995, p. 182) is the key to a life worth living, and that education is central to this quest. According to this view, for example, the life in the state of Nature (Rousseau), though it may be comfortable, is not worthwhile. Besides such purposes as reformation of society, rational control of one's self, and acquisition of useful knowledge and skills in life, the ideal of becoming aware of one's own situation and its hidden possibilities (hidden by custom, prejudice, social arrangement, or ignorance) emerged gradually as an important value that one should achieve through education. What is more, it is believed that the realization must be brought about by and for oneself. This seems to be one of the consistent themes of education, from the Enlightenment philosophers to contemporary theorists, though the ideas about what is required for such awareness only gradually evolved, and appreciation of imagination as a necessary part of it appeared much later.

As early as the 16th century, Michel de Montaigne (1580/1993) preferred wisdom to knowledge.[9] He thought that the capacity to use what one knows in order to make right decisions rather than mere book knowledge was more important. For example, regarding history, he wrote, "Let him be taught not so much the facts of history as how to judge them" (p. 62). His preference suggests that individuals must penetrate the stories and information given by others to see by themselves what situation and possibilities they have.

Educational philosophers in the 17th and 18th centuries such as Comenius, Locke, and Rousseau argued also against book learning, mere opinions, dependence on custom, or arbitrary authority and emphasized autonomous judgment based on one's firsthand knowledge.

Herbart in the 19th century thought that one of the major purposes of education was to create diverse interest in the students:

> It is of course a familiar precept that the teacher must try to arouse the interest of his pupils in all that he teaches. However, this precept is generally meant and understood to denote the idea that learning is the end and interest the means to attain it. I wish to reverse that relationship. Learning must *serve the purpose* of creating interest. Learning is transient, but interest must be lifelong. (quoted in Hilgenheger, 1993, pp. 7–8; italics in original)

All these views seem to point to an importance of awareness of one's lived situations and its untapped possibilities, or a sense that there is always more to see in the world. Although later generations critiqued some aspects of these writers' specific practical recommendations or philosophical assumptions, they seem to support, at least in principle, the basic educational value of awareness and understanding as a key to a worthwhile life.

These theorists, however, did not think that imaginativeness was a crucial part of the achievement of the basic value. It is in part because of their epistemology—their belief in the existence of objective knowledge and their assumption that sharpening the rational faculty (combined with senses) is all that is required in order to see objective knowledge. Flexibility of the mind and the playful/experimental attitude do not have much of a role in this scheme.

Some ideas that look like an appreciation of imagination or creativity are found in these early theorists. However, their appreciation of imagination is halfhearted, so to speak. For example, Herbart, along with Pestalozzi and others, appreciates the imagination as an image-making faculty, but his theory sees the imagination as a preparation for the formation of clear and distinct concepts. He was not so appreciative of the free play of imagination. Froebel, for another example, thought highly of creativity, but his idea of imagination and creativity was a symbol of divine nature embedded in the human nature that would develop by itself (as a seed grows into a flower as long as a proper environment is there) rather than something to be developed by such artificial means as instruction. He understood imagination or creativity as a manifestation of the divine seed in human beings, which is most lively in childhood.

The appreciation of imaginative capacity as it is conceived today emerged around the late 19th and early 20th century.[10] Dewey is a principal figure in this transition, or at least a figure who happened to work during that period and made arguments that were in line with what we understand to be the idea of imagination. Either way, Dewey is one of the authors most commonly referenced among the theorists of imagination today.

I do not mean to say that all educational theories of imagination today are the consequence of Deweyan pragmatism. However, they have a strong resonance with some aspects of it. The emphases on understanding (as opposed to mere knowledge), continuous and self-motivated learning, and alternative perspectives all indicate that a life worth living is not a matter of personal pleasure or comfort but a matter of awareness as a social being. And Dewey's understanding of the connection between imagination, rationality, and social life is one of the prototypical arguments that accommodate this perspective.

Therefore, we may safely say that the way we value imagination is a continuation of an important strand in modern education. Today, it is said that society may offer false choices; that there is no guarantee that one will reach any ultimate truth; and that there are diverse and competing perspectives, stories, values, and information in which one cannot simply tell truth from falsity. Nonetheless, somehow, one must be able to estimate one's situation reasonably accurately and see the possibility that things could be otherwise.

I do not mean to say that the connection between imagination and education, as I have described it so far, should be the only connection; I recognize the sociocultural contextuality of the view presented. Being aware of it, nonetheless, I suggest, first, that the picture I have drawn is a fairly reasonable summary of the general line of arguments among contemporary theorists of imaginative education and, second, that we should pursue this connection, because it is so tightly connected to the values we believe in.

The theory of imagination as it is discussed by contemporary scholars is interesting, because on the one hand, it is a continuation of the legacy of Western education from the Enlightenment, while on the other hand, it is trying to go somewhat beyond the scope of it, as seen in the rejection of some philosophical assumptions. Although some assumptions and language of the modern era may need to be critiqued and rejected, I do not believe the general project of education born in that era should be casually discarded.

## CONCLUSION

Although there are many competing views about what imagination means and why it is important for education, there seems to be a relatively stable center of concerns among the few theorists who regard imagination as educationally important. In this chapter, I presented what I understand to be one of the major centers of their concerns and suggested that it is a continuation of the project of modern Western education. Unless we are to discard the project itself, I believe, the development of imagination must be a necessary part of our education, and we have to work out how to implement it in practice as well as to clarify it conceptually.

It is impossible to identify the one defining characteristic of the idea of imagination; indeed, we do not need to. However, there should be justifiable reasons for taking up imagination seriously, and in these concluding remarks, I want to add one reason why I chose the term *imagination* over others with regard to its practical implications.

For me (here, I am taking a point of view as a classroom teacher), the choice of the term *imagination*, distinct from other similar concepts, particularly *creativity*, results at least in part from the sense of expectation it conveys. We sometimes apply the term *imaginative* to a person because we sense in him or her a potential or tendency to give effective surprise to people, and not to be tightly constrained by immediate actuality, standard procedure, or cliché. The idea of creativity, however, is too tightly connected to the idea of the product, but the idea of imagination is closer to the disposition of a person.

The idea of imagination also has a stronger connection to the idea of playful spirit. Being imaginative suggests being in pursuit of ideas driven by curiosity and fascination about the subject/task without being too concerned about the judgments of others; if the product happens to be judged excellent, it would be nice, but it is merely incidental.

As a symbol of the romantic spirit, imagination implies a rejection of the application of existing norms. In the context of classroom teaching, teachers sometimes intuitively think that some students have some imaginative potential even though these students are not particularly good in terms of scores and grades. It is very hard to justify such a judgment in light of commonly accepted criteria for excellence, but I do not think that this kind of intuitive judgment should be dismissed or repressed. This intuitive judgment is usually a reflection of the teacher's expectation that the children someday will blossom, maybe not in the precise subject the teacher is teaching, or even academically, and it justifies the teacher's effort not to give up on the children. Also the judgment makes the teacher reflect on, and sometimes revise, his or her own teaching method, curriculum, and requirements and give the children a little more flexible space in which to explore. Therefore, imagination in educational practice suggests an effort to become more mindful of what the student may be able to achieve and how the teacher may be able to make changes in assisting the student's quest.

As I have demonstrated, our conception of imagination has a strong connection with rationality. Imaginative rationality, so to speak, is a valuable thing to pursue, although we tend to think of rationality (and other educational values) in terms of something explicable (predominantly verbalizable and quantifiable). The idea of imagination implies existence of something that always escapes accepted norms, standards, and verbal description. While the emphasis on the product (as in the concept of creativity) suggests that we are able to evaluate the product (idea or object), the idea of imagination puts forth the sense that, even if we may not clearly explicate or evaluate it according to the accepted norms, we may find some possibilities for educational significance in what students exhibit; and this sense implies the need for exploration of hidden or not so obvious possibilities.

## NOTES

1. I will use *imagination*, *imaginativeness*, and *imaginative capacity* interchangeably.

2. For example, Rugg (1963) mentions Galileo's "*il lume naturale*," Gauss's "sudden lightning flash," Goethe's "daemonic voice," Whitehead's "prehension," and the common term "Ah ha!" (p. x). Also, Engell (1981/1999) examines uses, from the Latin *imaginatio* and Greek *phantasma*, Leibniz's *la puissance active* and *vis activa*, to the German *Einbildungskraft* and *Dichtkraft*.

3. Further, White (1990) writes, "An imaginative person is one with the ability to think of lots of possibilities, usually with some richness of detail" (p. 185). Egan draws very much on White in his definition of imagination. For similar definitions of imagination, see, for example, Dewey, 1933, p. 273 (imaginative as opposed to "the narrow effect of habituation"); Frye, 1963, p. 22; Warnock, 1976, p. 195; Hanson in Egan and Nadaner, 1988, p. 138; Singer and Singer, 1990, pp. 268–269; Johnson, 1993, p. 109; McCleary, 1993, pp. 50, 134; Bailin, 1994, p. 109; Greene, 1995, p. 19; Garrison, 1997, p. 77.

4. This kind of view on imagination did not change from Comenius in the 17th century (cf. Keatinge, 1901, pp. 6, 135) until the time of Herbart in the 19th century. Among major philosophers of education, Rousseau may be an interesting case to examine. While he appreciates the importance of imagination, for example, in morality (e.g., *Émile*, book 4, pp. 221, 223), he is opposed to arousing the imagination of a child (e.g., *Émile*, book 2, pp. 80–1).

5. Egan 1992, p. 30; White, 1990, pp. 184–185.

6. Barrow's view of imaginativeness has a strong emphasis on the product of thought rather than the process. For similar emphasis, see, for example, Bailin (1994).

7. For example, Noddings (1984) writes, "How good *I* can be is partly a function of how *you*—the other—receive and respond to me" (p. 6; italics in original).

8. See Raywid, 1981, which is a response to Noddings's paper. See also Noddings, 1984, pp. 171–172: "I reject the label [her view as affectivist] because such labels are often affixed simplistically, and the notion arises that one who insists on recognizing the affective base of morality must, therefore, minimize the role of cognitive activity."

9. Michele de Montaigne liked "a well-formed rather than a well-filled intellect" (p. 54).

10. Besides pragmatism's renewed notion of rationality, new psychological theories contributed to the appreciation of imagination. Vygotsky, for example, tried to get over a reductionistic view of the human mind in the early 20th century. He was interested in the higher mental functions, including imagination and creativity, which cannot be reduced to stimulus-response relations. Dewey, too, tried to get over "a false psychology" of "sensationalistic empiricism" (1985, pp. 33–34, 279).

*Chapter 3*

# Critical Thinking, Imagination, and New Knowledge in Education Research

## MAUREEN STOUT

In *The Pleasure of Finding Things Out,* physicist Richard Feynman writes that the responsibility of scientists is "to do what we can, learn what we can, improve the solutions and pass them on. . . . [I]f we suppress all discussion [we] doom man for a long time to the chains of authority, confined to the limits of our present imagination" (1999, pp. 149). His words are instructive, I believe, for social scientists as well as scientists, and especially for educators, since our work is most importantly about liberating the mind, allowing us to imagine—and realize—a future better than the present.

Part of realizing that future is ensuring the integrity of our research practices and the theories and paradigms that frame them, and in this chapter I argue that the progress of social science research, and in particular research in education, is, like scientific research, dependent upon both imagination and critical thinking. I will contend that critical thinking and imagination are not antithetical but are mutually supportive capacities essential to two domains of intellectual endeavor: knowledge building within a given field or theoretical framework (what I am calling intraparadigmatic knowledge building) and knowledge creation that challenges existing theoretical frameworks and provides the epistemological stimulus to develop new theories or paradigms (interparadigmatic knowledge building). I focus primarily on this latter domain here.

I begin by suggesting how imagination and critical thinking may be mutually enhancing by outlining how they have worked together to help us build knowledge that challenges existing paradigms and provides the critical, imaginative, and evaluative stimuli for new explanatory frameworks in science and education. I outline a few paradigm shifts in science and then turn to a specific theory change in education: that from modernism to postmodernism. I contend that the development of postmodern, post-liberal theories of education could not have occurred without imaginative, as well as critical, thinking. I conclude with suggestions for future research and outline some implications for teaching and curriculum.

My purpose here is not to identify the definitive relationship between critical thinking and imagination, or to insist that imagination is always useful or implicated in every critical intellectual exercise. I intend rather to illustrate that imagination may be more central to interparadigmatic knowledge building than we have heretofore realized—particularly as an evaluative capacity.

## PARADIGM PARTICULARS

Of course, since Thomas Kuhn first published *The Structure of Scientific Revolutions* in 1962, venturing into a discussion of paradigm shifts or theory change leads one into a minefield of competing conceptions about just what a paradigm is, and whether indeed it "shifts." (In fact, the phrase *theory change* was offered to me by a venerable colleague who suggested that *paradigm shift* was such a loaded term it was best to stay away from it altogether). In this discussion, however, I find paradigm shift the more useful phrase, since it best illustrates the kind of radical or revolutionary shift in thinking in which I am interested. But first, just what is a paradigm? For my purposes a paradigm is an explanatory framework, or perhaps collection of frameworks, that has become generally acknowledged and broadly used in a particular field as a useful theoretical and conceptual referent for much of the research in that field. I consider a paradigm a broader explanatory apparatus than a theory; in fact, a paradigm may encompass several theories.

There may be several paradigms coexisting in a particular field, although at any given time, one paradigm may predominate. As I discuss in more detail later on, the postmodern paradigm has arguably been the dominant paradigm in education research for at least the past 15 years (and perhaps much longer). Leaving aside arguments regarding whether it is merely a reaction to modernism or truly a new paradigm, it is clear that in education research and in social science research generally, modernism now has a clear competitor.

For the purposes of this discussion, I will use Kuhn's (1970) interpretation of paradigm shifts as a usable model. According to Kuhn, the process of knowledge building within a paradigm continues as long as new knowledge can be adequately assimilated into it, and as long as the paradigm retains its explanatory integrity. But when the preponderance of anomalies in the paradigm stretch it beyond its original explanatory powers and purposes, researchers will shift their efforts from preserving the paradigm to developing and supporting a new one.

There are, however, many other explanations of how science progresses, including those of Karl Popper, Imre Lakatos, and Paul Feyerabend. If we put all these observers on a continuum, we might have Popper on one end, representing the realists, then Lakatos, then Kuhn, and finally Feyerabend on the other end, representing the radical relativist (or "anarchist") position (Casti, 1989, p. 36). Lakatos contended that just because a certain hypothesis has been refuted does not mean that scientists will discard a theory and leap into the epistemological unknown to try to develop a new one. They will first revise peripheral rules or concepts, and it is only when the core concepts are threatened that a paradigm is in danger of collapse (Noddings, 1995, p. 123). I like to call this the "sinking ship" theory: Adherents of a particular paradigm will hold on to it until it looks like it may become epistemologically and politically (and professionally) untenable—and only then jump toward a new one.

Whether or not we accept Kuhn's or others' interpretations of paradigm shifts in toto, a couple of things are clear: Researchers work within recognized paradigms and new paradigms are created to challenge or replace existing ones. The question that challenges us here is what the role of imagination might be in this development of new paradigms.

I would suggest that the transformation from one paradigm to another develops over time through reasoned discussion and analysis but that the period (be it short or long) when there is a shift in allegiance from one paradigm to another is also imaginative in nature because it involves the recognition of the contingency of present and future life—that life could and can be otherwise. Developing or attaching to a new paradigm requires the intellectual, psychological, and even moral courage to go beyond the accepted confines of the dominant paradigm to challenge not only the subject or content of that paradigm but the explanatory integrity of the paradigm itself. One difference between those who cling to the sinking ship and those who save themselves is that the latter can imagine the explanatory and epistemological capacities of a new paradigm and embrace its challenge. Whether the new paradigm will stay afloat is another matter entirely, of course, but creating or adopting a new paradigm requires not only reason and logic but also imagination—the catalyst for change.

## THINKING—CRITICALLY AND IMAGINATIVELY

Before looking at the role of imagination and critical thinking in paradigm shifts, we need to clarify what we mean by critical thinking and imagination and the possible relationship between them. Harvey Siegel (1988, p. 34) defines critical thinking as principled thinking. The critical thinker seeks reasons on which to base her judgments and in seeking reasons, she is committing herself to principles (p. 33). I call these principles intellectual values: fairness, consistency, impartiality, the desire to search for the truth, and so forth. The critical thinker rejects arbitrariness, uses acknowledged standards and criteria for evaluating arguments and making judgments, and provides warranted support of arguments and beliefs. Critical thinking is thus a deliberate kind of thinking that uses publicly acknowledged and publicly defensible principles. In Siegel's words, a critical thinker is one who is "appropriately moved by reasons"(p. 32).

I agree with Bailin and colleagues (Bailin, Case, Coombs, & Daniels, 1999a), however, that critical thinking is not just a set of generic skills that can be used in any situation. They argue that "there are no good grounds for supposing that terms like comparing, classifying and inferring denote mental processes which one can improve through repetition" (1999, p. 280). They further contend that to become critical thinkers we need background knowledge and familiarity with concepts within a particular area, as well as effective heuristics and habits of mind (p. 285). Critical thinking may involve problem solving, assessing standards, applying principles—indeed a variety of skills, procedures, or attitudes—but these will likely differ qualitatively in each context.

In other words, while I think it is reasonable to say that one must always use good reasons in argumentation and critical thinking, what counts as good reasons may differ from one context to another. Robin Barrow (1990, p. 91) agrees, noting that a critical thinker is one who understands not only the rules of good reasoning, but also the form they take in certain kinds of inquiry and understanding and knows how to use them appropriately in relation to various kinds of subject matter. Siegel (1998) emphasizes, however, I think rightly, that a critical thinker must also have a good grasp of the *nature* of reasons, warrant, and justification as general concepts across all fields.

Siegel also notes that there are certain dispositions required for being a critical thinker. The critical thinker must be *willing* to use appropriate reasons and principles and use them accordingly. Siegel calls this the "critical spirit," and I believe that having that critical spirit means being willing to submit one's own reasoning and judgments to rigorous, principled evaluation by oneself and others. Having a critical disposition is, essentially, an affective component of reasoning, and Siegel (1998) notes that conceptions of a reasonable person "as one without emotion, and as one who "turns off" her emotions while engaging in reason, are untenable." What I have termed *intellectual skills* Siegel calls "rational passions," and concludes that "the critical thinker must *care* about reason and its use"(1998, p. 40).

This conception of the critical thinker as one who consciously employs her emotions while reasoning and who consciously evaluates her own thinking and that of others links us to imagination. As Kieran Egan and Keiichi Takaya describe in their chapters in the present volume, the concept of imagination has a long and lively history. I will leave that history in their capable hands and begin here with Egan's (1992a) definition of imagination as the capacity to think of things as possibly being so, as an intentional act of mind, as a capacity that enriches rationality and is the source of invention, novelty, and generativity (p. 47).

Imagination for Egan has affective components, since it is implicated in perception, in bodily experience, in image-forming, and in generating new experiences and ideas. It is not merely idle fancy or romantic daydreaming, although I believe that daydreaming, conjecturing, and even hypothesizing might also be considered imaginative exercises.

Imagination, has, therefore, roots in both the affective and cognitive domains. Thus the rigid separation that we have historically identified between reason and emotion or the intellect and the imagination is, I believe, misguided. Indeed, imagination may be the bridge that crosses these two domains, enhancing both. As Egan (1992a) points out:

> Identifying imagination in the capacity to think of something as possibly being so, certainly does not suggest any conflict with rationality. Rather, the ability to hold alternative conceptions in the mind and assess their adequacy or appropriateness would seem a necessary component of any sophisticated rational activity. (p. 42)

Mark Johnson (1993) agrees. In *Moral Imagination* he notes that "we have been taught to regard imagination . . . as a subjective, free-flowing, creative process not governed by any rules or constrained by any rationally defined concepts" (p. 2), but he contends that the rigid separation of reason from imagination is erroneous because there is no such thing as pure rationality separate from the psychological, emotional, historical, and political constraints that govern any instance of moral reasoning (p. 3).

We might begin to conceptualize imagination, then, as part of critical thinking itself—the part that allows us to view the world and our place(s) in it from a new, heretofore unexamined position. As Maxine Greene (1995, p. 19) explains, imagination is an acknowledgment of the contingency of our current lives that allows us to imagine possibilities for our future lives; an ability "to look at things as if they could be otherwise." For Greene, imagination is critical for students to envision a better future for themselves and is thus a personally and politically liberating force, as well as an affective and intellectual one. I will argue that imagination can also be an epistemologically subversive force, helping us generate radically new forms of knowledge.

If imagination permits us to view the world in new ways it will thus, by definition, provide us with the impetus for assessing that world and our new perspective on it. That capacity for seeing what might be, what is not easily visible, or, as the postmodernists would put it, the "other," is, I would argue, an evaluative capacity. In *Imagination in Teaching and Learning*, Kieran Egan (1992a) refers to this capacity, noting that the intellectual flexibility that seems to be central to imaginativeness helps us

> conceive of a wider than normal range of states or actions that do not exist or that do not follow by literal extrapolation from current states or actions or from conventional representations of states or actions. In conceiving an indeterminate range of such states or actions the imaginative person can hold them in the mind, consider potential implications, assess their appropriateness, or scan their features, selecting whichever might be most unusual and effective. (p. 37)

As an evaluative capacity, imagination can help us separate from ourselves and our daily experience and shed new and critical light upon the human experience—something artists, for example, do every day. And of course that opportunity to see ourselves in a unique and critical light—whether it be to see alternatives for research or for living our lives—has affective as well as intellectual consequences, since opportunity means choice, and making choices—whether professional or personal—is always an emotional event.

We begin to see, therefore, that imagination and critical thinking may be conceptualized as mutually supportive capacities. Imagination may even be considered a necessary part of critical thinking itself. In *The Educational Imagination*, Elliot Eisner (1985) explores the role of what we might call *critical imagination* in the conceptualization; implementation; and, particularly, evaluation of curriculum. Eisner proposes a new approach to evaluation based on a concept of *educational connoisseurship* in which teachers and researchers attend to and assess the daily "happenings of educational life in a focused, sensitive, and conscious way" (p. 221). He believes that a connoisseurship approach to evaluation will help us get to the essence of what goes on in classrooms, avoid mechanistic and test-driven assessment strategies, and allow us to develop new theories and models from which to view current issues in education. Educational connoisseurship is, for Eisner, subjective and aesthetically driven, but it is also a critical act, involving description, interpretation, and assessment (pp. 223–235).

In sum, when we consider the affective component of critical thinking (the "critical spirit") and of imagination (the experiencing of new possibilities) and the centrality of the evaluative capacity in both critical thinking (through assessment of warrant and reasons) and imagination (through helping us hypothesize about what might be), it seems reasonable to suggest that imagination and critical thinking are closely allied, at least in these areas.

When we think imaginatively and critically, we explore the familiar in unusual ways and the unusual in familiar ways. Imagination can help us ask new questions about current issues in education and help us identify new issues that need to be examined, while critical thinking provides the tools to pursue these questions in a rational, deliberate way. Indeed, as Bailin and colleagues (Bailin, Case, Coombs, & Daniels, 1999b) note, critical thinking "often requires imagining possible consequences, generating original approaches and identifying alternative perspectives" (p. 288).

Imagination may also suggest to us new ways to evaluate concepts and practices in education research and enhance the tools of critical thinking by allowing us to reflect on our use of those tools. Logical reasoning, for example, requires imagination because it requires us to work in the hypothetical, but then we need to be able not only to identify logical steps to their conclusion, but also imagine alternative conclusions and examine them. Imagination is a capacity that, like critical thinking, is not only generative of knowledge, but also (as Robin Barrow [1990] argues) based on knowledge, since it presupposes the ability to distinguish between the real, the possible, and the impossible (pp. 94–95).

Imagination is, I believe, the capacity that allows us to develop metaskills—such as evaluation—which are required for us to assess the form, methods, and content of knowledge within and between paradigms. Imagination is also essential in the "generating of the possible"—and that generation is, I will argue, the root of new knowledge and new paradigms. We might say that critical thinking allows us to examine ideas and arguments within defined theoretical and paradigmatic boundaries and imagination helps us examine those boundaries. In other words, critical thinking helps us think clearly within the box and imagination allows us to think outside it—and evaluate it.

As we see in the sections that follow, building new knowledge requires critical thinking and logical reasoning skills but also something like an "imaginative leap" into the epistemological unknown. This leap (or stumble, or crawl) involves going just beyond where rational analysis may take us, but we then use reason to analyze where we are, to determine whether we have landed in a field fertile with epistemological bounty, or in something that yields only muddy beliefs and tangled myths. I examine a few of these "leaps" below.

## IMAGINATION IN SCIENTIFIC REVOLUTIONS

We will recall that for Kuhn (1970) a paradigm shift occurs when the existing paradigm no longer serves its original explanatory function. He explains the process thusly:

> Discovery commences with the awareness of anomaly, i.e. with the recognition that nature has somehow violated the paradigm-induced expectations that govern normal science. It then continues with a more or less extended exploration of the area of anomaly. And it closes only when the paradigm theory has been adjusted so that the anomalous has become the expected. (p. 53)

Or as he explains more parsimoniously, new facts or phenomena discovered in a game governed by a particular set of rules then require the elaboration of another set (p. 52).

However researchers and philosophers of science frame it, it is clear that there is knowledge building and paradigm construction (and deconstruction) in science. It is also clear that these activities require critical thinking as I have described it above: the use of good reasons, knowledge of a discipline and context (to determine what good reasons are), respect for the use of evidence, rational deliberation, and so on. Critical thinking is essential to science, since it is at the root of the scientific method: observing, hypothesizing, experimenting, and testing, leading to the creation of laws and theories. This is not, I think, a claim that will incite much debate. It may, however, raise some eyebrows if I suggest that the revolutionary (or non-normal) science that leads to paradigm shifts requires the use of imagination as well.

This brings us to the essence of what science is about—and why knowledge building and paradigm construction are in form and process essentially the same in the sciences and the social sciences. In high school some of us thought that science was either about techniques—doing experiments that often involved unpleasant tasks such as taking apart the eyeball of a pig, or seemingly irrelevant tasks such as balancing equations in chemistry. But the reason we thought that was not because that is what science is about, but because we were never taught that it's really about ideas. As John Casti (1989) writes, the cataloguing of facts is not the essence of science (p. 11); nor is science primarily concerned with finding answers. It—like all fields of inquiry—is about studying ideas and developing a deep understanding of them (p. 12).

Imagination, as much as any other capacity, helps us identify new and exciting ideas, as when a significant discovery is made or a new theory or paradigm is developed. And some observers contend that in fact the greatest discoveries are made using imagination, or when one is truly "thinking outside the box." Gerald Holton, in *The Advancement of Science, and Its Burdens* (1986), notes that Einstein questioned everything that had become familiar or that had the stamp of scientific approval—a cultural characteristic shared by other great thinkers, such as Copernicus, Galileo, Darwin, and Freud (p. 91)—and that Einstein referred to the fundamentals of science as initially "free inventions of the human mind" that were "purely fictional in character"(p. 121). In a fascinating chapter entitled "Einstein and the Shaping of Our Imagination," Holton (1986) writes that the most creative scientists,

> almost by definition, do not build their constructs patiently by assembling blocks that have been precast by others and certified as sound. On the contrary, they . . . melt down the ready-made materials of science at hand and recast them in a way that their contemporaries tend to think is outrageous. (p. 115)

Einstein, writes Holton, gave his loyalty

> primarily to his own belief system rather than to the current faith; by perceiving and exploiting the man-made nature and plasticity of human conceptions; by demonstrating eventually that the new unity he has promised does become lucid and convincing to the lesser mortals active in his field—that he has it all "wrong" in the right way; and, in those rare cases, by even issuing ideas that lend themselves, quite apart from misuse and oversimplification, to further adaptation and transformation in the imagination of similarly exalted spirits who live on the other side of disciplinary boundaries. (p. 116)

Whereas we normally consider Einstein as exemplifying scientific thinking, Holton suggests that imagination, as well as moral courage, also characterized Einstein's challenges to modern scientific thought.

The Copernican revolution and the discovery of DNA are also examples of revolutionary epistemological developments that may be seen as the result of critical thinking and imagination. In *The Rhetoric of Science* (1990), Alan Gross notes that the shift from the Ptolemaic to the Copernican paradigm, although not without narrative preparation and argumentative justification, still came as a shock and an irrational claim to many in the scientific community at the time and for more than a century Copernicanism had few adherents. Rheticus, Copernicus's student, attempted to justify the shift as a natural outgrowth of Ptolemaic astronomy, but he couldn't make the argument stick, and thus, Gross writes, the change to heliocentricity was as much a force of will as of reason (pp. 101–107). Here imagination—of what might be—and force of will took up where reason left off. That does not undermine Copernicus's theory at all. On the contrary, it suggests that his contemporaries did not have his vision, and could not *imagine* what he could, at the time. It is important to note that his imaginings were not, again, idle fancy, but part of an emotional and intellectual leap to just outside where reason took him, but to where reason—and theory—eventually caught up.

Similarly, of the conclusion by Oswald Avery and his colleagues in 1944 that genes were made of DNA, Nobel laureate Salvador Luria (1986) writes:

> No pressure or competition or sudden emergence of irrefutable data precipitated the decision to publish. . . . He exhibited . . . a willingness to impose on a still confused mass of data a certainty that is emotional as well as rational. Such a source of certainty in science is unrecognizable by those who believe certainty comes only after innumerable controls and attempts to disprove. The certainty Avery exhibited is more akin to illumination, a sudden vision projecting the possibility of an intellectual leap. (pp. 29–30)

In each of these instances, the shift from one scientific paradigm to another can be considered as much an emotional, risk-taking exercise as an expression of critical thinking. This does not mean that there were not years—even decades—of research, argumentation, and experimentation behind each but that when push came to shove, it required a force of will, an intellectual leap, or even perhaps an act of faith to stand up for a new way of thinking about the physical world. The essence of these paradigmatic changes—shifts that have forever changed our view of humanity in the world—is about ideas, based in critical thinking, but engendered by imagination.

It is no different in education research. Whereas the areas and methodology of inquiry may differ, the overall research endeavor is essentially the same: exploring problems and trying to develop broad theoretical schemata (paradigms) that help us understand them.

## THE STORY OF A PARADIGM SHIFT

Perhaps the most significant paradigm shift in education in this century is the challenge to modern liberal theory and its claim of equal opportunity, and the consequent shift to postmodern critical theory. I will not attempt to explore all aspects of this shift, for as Pauline Rosenau (1992) writes in *Postmodernism and the Social Sciences* (see pp. 5–6). postmodernism criticizes almost everything that modernism has engendered—industrialization, the accumulation of Western civilization, liberal democracy, tolerance, egalitarianism, the possibility of neutrality and objectivity rationality (in research and in life), and metanarratives (to name only a few things). I am interested primarily in one of liberalism's core principles: equal opportunity, and specifically equal educational opportunity, since I believe that it is the apparent failure of liberalism to fulfill the promises of equality that led, in large part, to the rise of postmodernism in education.

Since the 17th and 18th centuries, from the writings of John Locke and Jean-Jacques Rousseau to contemporary thinkers such as John Rawls and Charles Taylor, the idea of individuals contracting with one another to form a civil society has been a central focus of liberal theory. Defining the relationship of individuals to one another and to the state, and defining their rights and responsibilities in those relationships, remain a core interest not only for philosophers, but also for researchers in education, since public schooling is perhaps the principal vehicle through which common political and social values are transmitted.

One of those core values, and arguably the central tenet of modern liberal theory, is that each individual should have rights equal to those of all other individuals. Indeed the promises of modernism—progress and opportunity—are built on this ideal of equality of opportunity for all in a meritocratic society. But as we will see, a cursory glance at the history of the past 200 years or more in the United States and Canada will tell us that this ideal has not become reality. Despite constitutional guarantees respecting the rights of persons, and legal cases such as *Brown v. the Board of Education of Topeka, Kansas,* that should have ensured the death of inequality, many individuals and groups have experienced inequality of opportunity based on race, ethnicity, gender, disability, and—after 9/11—even country of origin. Twentieth-century observers have examined liberalism and found it wanting, claiming with unimpeachable logic that a theory that promises to provide equal opportunity for all but provides it to only a select few isn't providing equal opportunity—period. And along with the many other criticisms of modern liberalism that Rosenau outlines, this criticism provided the impetus for the creation of the postmodern paradigm of education.

As I have suggested, a paradigm shift is not merely an intellectual transformation, but an emotional one as well. In this instance, it also has several facets. It begins with a conceptual change: a change in how minorities are viewed in North America. With this conceptual shift goes a change in the language we use to describe minority individuals. Then schooling practices, public policy, and laws change and education research begins to reflect those developments. New theories subsequently develop from this process to challenge existing theories of equality in society and finally a new paradigm develops that demands that we reconceptualize not only equality, but also our definitions of "self" and "minority" in a multicultural society.

Until well into this century, in both the United States and Canada, many persons of color were considered less important, or somehow less valuable, than White persons. Individuals and groups we now refer to as "indigenous" or "aboriginal" or "First Nations" were considered in anthropological terms "savages," in legal and ethical terms "nonpersons," and in political terms, disenfranchised (literally). The famous case of *Plessy v. Ferguson* in 1895 enshrined this in the United States. Homer Plessy, who was one eighth African American and seven eighths White, was arrested for refusing to ride in the colored section of a train. The Supreme Court, in examining the case, determined that segregated facilities could exist if they were equal. Thus the "separate but equal" doctrine was born.

It took until 1954 and *Brown v. the Board of Education* for "separate but equal" to be thrown out. This case, probably the most important in the history of the fight for civil rights in the United States, determined that segregated facilities, in this case, schools, were, by definition, unequal. These cases and the history that surrounds them are well known, but how can we explain the Court's complete change in perspective over those 50-odd years? The legal referent for each was the same: the 14th Amendment to the Constitution, ratified in 1868, which declares: "No State shall make . . . any law which shall abridge the privileges . . . nor deprive any person of life, liberty, or property, without due process of law; nor deny to any person within its jurisdiction the equal protection of the laws"(Spring, 2000, 118).

Of course courts are composed of individuals, who, leaving aside their experience and understanding of the law and their oath to uphold it, are, as Mark Johnson (1993) reminded us, nonetheless making legal (and in this case, moral) decisions within particular psychological, political, and historical contexts. And for each of those justices, the contexts are different. Thus we may try to explain this shift in perspective by saying that no two groups of 12 people will adjudicate the same issue the same way; or we could simply say it was just the way it went. But the *Brown* decision is historic precisely because it reflects a fundamental change in values and attitudes toward African Americans in the United States.

Slavery is only possible if the enslaved—the "other," in postmodern terms—are considered nonpersons. "Separate but equal" is only possible if those segregated are considered less important than the majority. Thus in order for *Brown* to occur, a significant shift in the concept of minorities—and the concept of the individual—had to take place. It required, in part, the imaginative capacity for envisioning a different conception and different life for a group of persons who had heretofore not even been considered persons. It also meant that the self-identity (as well as the public identity) of Blacks in America would be transformed. Of course this shift did not take place in an instant, and it occurred in a context of significant changes in the economic, political, and educational status of Blacks in America.

But it is a huge conceptual and imaginative shift—and an expression of moral courage—from identifying a group of persons by their skin color, and identifying them as less than full persons, to determining that that group can no longer be limited by color, and indeed that their rights as full persons must be inviolate.

Along with this gradual change in image and concept came a change in language, policy, and practice with respect to Blacks. The word *nigger* became unacceptable. It was replaced by *colored,* then *Black,* and then *African American* (although there is still some discussion among members of the group as to whether Black or African American is preferable). The terms used reflect and cement the change in image, as did the legal changes that followed, such as the 1964 Civil Rights Act, busing of students to enforce desegregation in schools, and most recently the somewhat controversial practice of affirmative action. But the most important part of this change is the idea that individuals have the right to determine what group, if any, they belong to and how that group shall be named.

Following these conceptual changes, public school policy and practice also changed. Magnet schools were created, intended to provide a high-quality and at times specialized education that would attract both White and Black students, thereby fostering "natural" desegregation. Curricula began to include the history, language, and experience of minority students. Academic research on all aspects of the minority experience in public schools exploded in the 1960s and continues to this day, addressing everything from teaching methods to continued segregation, tracking, and evaluation and curriculum—indeed all aspects of public education.

From Adorno and Horkheimer of the Frankfurt School and John Dewey in the early part of the century to Gramsci, Freire, and others, the criticism of the failure of liberalism to provide equal opportunity offered a fertile ground for the development of radical, multicultural, and postmodern theories of education. These theories claim to encompass a language of possibility not only from the literal chains of economic, educational, and social oppression, but also from the epistemological tethers of liberal theories that promise much, but, it is charged, deliver little.

Adorno and Horkheimer worried that liberal ideals, while emphasizing equality, liberty, and progress, were just another ideology that tethers the individual, while making that person think he or she is free. Contemporary observers, such as Peter McLaren, Ira Shor, Henry Giroux, Stanley Aronowitz, Michael Apple, and bell hooks, tackle inequality through a variety of critical, poststructural, postmodern, neo-Marxist, and feminist approaches and also continue Adorno and Horkheimer's critique, arguing that liberalism, like all "metanarratives," is based on an unproblematized conception of self that ultimately enslaves the individual, while promising him or her liberation. These theorists contend, among other things, that we need to go beyond claims for simple equality and bring in notions of power and difference into theory and practice, and that the lived experiences, language, and histories of oppressed groups must be part of any conception of equality of opportunity and social justice.

In *Life in Schools*, Peter McLaren (1994) laments the state of North American public schools, arguing that "freedom and equality have become dust-covered relics in history's warehouse" (p. 4). He is as critical of neoliberal accounts of schooling, which, he contends, have been incapable of addressing the major problems that schools face, as he is of neoconservatives in the 1980s, who argued for a return to traditional values, character education, and the dismantling of affirmative action. As Charles Taylor (1992) points out, the charge leveled by observers such as McLaren is that "blind" liberalisms (those that advocate equal treatment irrespective of difference) are themselves the reflection of particular cultures and that therefore, the supposedly fair society is, almost by definition, highly discriminatory.

The core components of this paradigm shift can be summarized as follows: First, the practice of separate but equal was rejected; second, liberal theory and its promise of equality of opportunity were rediscovered as important principles; third, in the apparent absence of equal opportunity, liberalism was evaluated and found wanting; and fourth, postmodern theory developed from this critique of modern liberalism. I have made this story brief for the sake of clarity, but it is important to remember that these are enormous intellectual and emotional shifts. The field of education has been transformed from one in which students of color were ignored to one in which they are front and center, and from which concerns about equality were tangential to one in which they are absolutely critical.

In addition, evaluating a theory (liberalism) that was so much part of the fabric of society that it was almost invisible requires being able in some sense to stand outside the current paradigm and examine it. And going beyond current thinking and envisioning a world where all might really have equal opportunity involves imagination, the capacity that helps us see things as they might be and as they are in new ways. Finally, proposing an entirely new way of looking at the world is surely a feat of imagination as well as of critical thinking.

Only something akin to an intellectual leap can allow us to think outside the confines of the modernist paradigm and challenge its core assumptions. Without the postmodernists we may never have recognized modernism as a metanarrative at all. Most important, perhaps, postmodernism has questioned our concept of the self in society, proposing that notions of identity and self in society are far more complex than we might think. Here we see how imagination can be epistemologically subversive, in helping us question the foundations of accepted knowledge, and thereby lay the groundwork for the creation of new knowledge.

But a new paradigm cannot itself be immune to criticism. I will note in passing that one may identify any number of limitations of postmodern education theory: for example, it may be only a critique of modernism and not a new paradigm; alternatively, it may be itself a metanarrative; it may depend too much on notions of power, and most of it is, unarguably, written in language that is too arcane for those it is meant to help and many others to understand. Postmodern theorists themselves must use the same imaginative and critical thinking they applied to liberalism to examine their own theory and clarify its guiding principles—before it implodes, like a black hole, under the massive weight of epistemological nothingness.

But whatever its merits or shortcomings, postmodern education theory has made us call into question our fundamental political and educational ideals and help us see liberal theory in new ways. Whether we adopt this new vision is up to each of us, but gaining a fresh perspective on equality in theory and practice can only strengthen our understanding of it. And if we recall Lakatos's point that it is when the core concepts of a paradigm are threatened that a paradigm is in danger of collapsing, then liberals would be well advised to pay attention to their critics.

## IMPLICATIONS FOR RESEARCH AND TEACHING

I have claimed that imagination and critical thinking are both implicated in paradigm development and evaluation. Together they can be a revolutionary, and not just evolutionary, force in social science—and education—research. Imaginative thinking is also courageous thinking, since it demands that we evaluate the limitations of our preferred research theories and methods. As Stanley Aronowitz and Henry Giroux (1985) argue in *Education Under Siege*, "If we want a creative citizenry that is capable of constituting itself as a democratic public sphere, then curriculum and school organizations must address the imaginary, and refrain from finding techniques to displace it by fear to the prevailing order"(p. 20). In other words, we must not be afraid of venturing into the unknown, since that is where we can explore possibilities for improving our lives—and the lives of our students. As Maxine Greene (1995) reminds us: "Once we can see our givens as contingencies, then we may have an opportunity to posit alternative ways of living and valuing and to make choices" (p. 23).

But if what I have argued is the case, what does this mean for research and teaching? It suggests that we can only advance knowledge by continually examining not only our work in a particular paradigm but that paradigm itself. In fact, it seems to me that continual evaluation of the adequacy of a paradigm at any given moment is essential if we wish to assess its explanatory capacities; to determine if those capacities are adequate; and how, when, or if it is time to develop alternatives to it. Such analysis of topic as well as method and theory would seem to require the flexibility of thinking, generativity, and evaluative skills that suggest imaginative as well as critical thinking.

One difficulty in examining paradigm shifts is, of course, trying to determine where one is at the current historical moment. Are we in a truly postmodern age? Is postmodern education theory a fad or does it offer true liberty and progress (fine modern notions)? These are important questions— but for another day. I do believe that as a result of the postmodern challenge, modernism—and modern liberal conceptions of schooling and inequality— have been reinvigorated. But in terms of the process of revolutionary knowledge-building, which has been the focus of this chapter, I believe there may have been an initial conceptual shift to postmodern thought but there is now a tension between them as if they were balanced on a seesaw. Who knows how the balance will shift in the future? Perhaps the most important point for this discussion is that it is essential to be aware of these theoretical tensions, constraints, limitations—and possibilities—and that such awareness is only possible if we exercise our imagination as well as our reason.

Of course this theoretical balance beam may mean that we are in the uncomfortable position of existing between incommensurable or competing paradigms. A positive outcome of this, however, is that education researchers are required to inquire more imaginatively into our own research, examine our theoretical assumptions, our reasons for inquiry, our methods, our intended outcomes, our use of research, and our claims for its relevance in education. In fact, I would argue that if a paradigm remains dominant for an extended period, it may be a sign that the research community at large is lacking in imagination—the imagination to evaluate it as new (anomalous) knowledge and new insights arise that challenge it.

In terms of teaching, we must foster imaginative thinking and critical thinking in public schools, to ensure the epistemological health of scientific and social scientific research. Classwork that requires filling in blanks or getting the "right" answers on a multiple choice test are not the kinds of exercises that will develop these skills. We must affirm imagination and critical thinking as priorities in our classrooms. There are innumerable capacities that may come under the rubric of *critical thinking*, including developing lateral as well as vertical thinking, identifying assumptions in arguments, generating questions about a text or argument, working on open-ended and closed problems, and the tools we identified earlier: consistency, impartiality, using acknowledged standards and criteria for evaluating arguments, and providing warranted support of arguments and beliefs.

I have argued that imagination and critical thinking work in tandem in knowledge building, and therefore as teachers we need to, as Maxine Greene (1995) notes, "pose questions, [to] seek out explanations, [to] look for reasons, [to] construct meaning"(p. 24). By doing this, she says, the teacher helps the student (and him- or herself) "move from the habitual and ordinary" to the unusual, the unexpected, and maybe even the miraculous. Again, recalling Harvey Siegel's (1988) arguments, it requires not only skills but also the disposition to develop those skills. Matthew Lippmann's Philosophy for Children is one example of a program that helps foster these dispositions and Kieran Egan's (1997) conception of teaching, described in *The Educated Mind*, illustrates how to ensure that the imagination is implicated in all aspects of the learning process.

Finally, one of the most important implications of this discussion is that it highlights the importance of developing evaluative skills. In Bloom's taxonomy, evaluation is the highest level of cognition, and I believe that if critical thinking and logical analysis are the foundation of evaluation, imagination is its inspiration. Imagination allows us to hypothesize about what is possible; critical thinking helps us reason through those possibilities, and evaluation both helps us assess the quality of those processes and tells us whether our hypothesizing and reasoning are directed toward productive ends.

In this chapter I have argued that critical thinking and imaginative thinking are mutually enhancing skills and that both are necessary for interparadigmatic knowledge building within education and within the social sciences generally. Although I have discussed critical thinking and imaginative thinking as conceptually separate, I believe that the next step in research should be to reformulate a conception of critical thinking that incorporates imagination as a central capacity of that thinking.

## CONCLUSION

I will conclude where I began, with Richard Feynman (1999): "It is our responsibility as scientists . . . to teach how doubt is not to be feared but welcomed and discussed, and to demand this freedom as our duty to all coming generations. . . . If we want to solve a problem that we have never solved before, we must leave the door to the unknown ajar" (p. 149). And that door is opened by imagination.

*Part II*

# Imagination
# and
# Educational Practices

*Chapter 4*

# Affect and Cognition Reunited in the Mathematics Classroom: The Role of the Imagination

## PETER LILJEDAHL

What is the role of the imagination in the "doing" of mathematics? Is such a question even answerable? In this chapter I will engage in a somewhat free-ranging discussion of the role of the imagination in the specific instances of mathematical problem solving. Before I begin, however, it may be prudent for me to first discuss exactly what it is I am looking for in my meandering over the mathematical landscape. What exactly is imaginative mathematics? To answer this without first defining *imaginative* is somewhat presumptuous. Let me just state that it is my goal to demonstrate that some forms of mathematical thinking have within them an aspect of the imagination, and of those experiences some have it more than others.

### DOING MATHEMATICS: PROBLEM SOLVING AND INVENTION

I begin with an anecdote. Picture if you will someone in the grips of "doing" mathematics. There he sits, slightly unkempt, madly scribbling away on a pad of paper in some unintelligible language of symbols and diagrams (Kasner & Newman, 1940). The desk in his small office is in danger of being lost under the mountain of papers and books covered in similar scribbles. Occasionally he will break from his frantic writing to pace the room, mumbling to himself, perhaps making a few notations on a chalkboard before returning to his overburdened desk. This may be a Hollywood exaggeration of the nature of mathematical activity but the image is not unfounded (see, for example, the case of Andrew Wiles and Fermat's Last Theorem in Singh, 1997).

My purpose in painting the preceding picture, however, was not to comment on the eccentric nature of Hollywood mathematicians, but to accentuate an ambiguity. Was the scene described one of a mathematician inventing new mathematics or of a student solving a mathematical problem? Are they different? On a global scale they are. A mathematician forging ahead into the uncharted territory of the mathematical landscape is going where no one has gone before. A student diligently working at completing some challenging task set by his or her mathematics teacher is likely venturing down a much traveled path. On a local scale, however, there is no difference. Both the research mathematician and the student are working in unfamiliar territory; "between the work of a student who tries to solve a problem in geometry or algebra and a work of invention, one can say there is only a difference of degree" (Hadamard, 1954, p. 104). As such, it could just as easily be said that the mathematician is solving a problem for the field of mathematics as the student is inventing new mathematics for him- or herself. That is, for many purposes, mine included, mathematical problem solving and mathematical invention are indistinguishable. So, I will treat them as such, each implying the other.

Having narrowed the focus of my discussion down to mathematical problem solving I will now explore two very distinct, and opposite, problem solving processes: design and creativity.

## PROBLEM SOLVING BY DESIGN

In a general sense, *design* is defined as the algorithmic and deductive approach to solving a problem (Rusbult, 2000). The process begins with a clearly defined goal or objective from which point there is a great reliance on relevant past experience, referred to as repertoire (Bruner, 1964; Schön, 1987), to produce possible options that will lead toward a solution of the problem (Poincaré, 1952). These options are then examined through a process of conscious evaluations (Dewey, 1933) to determine their suitability for advancing the problem toward the final goal. In very simple terms, problem solving by design is the process of deducing the solution from that which is already known. This may seem an oversimplification, but if you examine any problem-solving heuristics (Burton, 1984; Mason, Burton, & Stacey, 1982; Polya 1957), it becomes clear that it is an accurate one.

However, many would consider a problem that can be solved by such means to not be worthy of the title *problem*. Resnick and Glaser (1976) define a problem as being something that you do not have the experience to solve. As such, a repertoire of past experiences sufficient for dealing with such a "problem" would disqualify it from the ranks of "problems" and relegate it to that of "exercises." Mathematicians, in general, also do not see such "problems" as being problematic. Dan Kleitman makes the comment that "any problem in which you can see how to attack it by deliberate effort, is a routine problem, and cannot be an important discovery" (quoted in Liljedhal, 2004, p. 98). He goes on to specify that to solve a true problem "you must try and fail by deliberate efforts, and then rely on a sudden inspiration or intuition or if you prefer to call it luck." The sudden inspiration that Kleitman speaks of is that flash of insight that suddenly appears, often when least expected, and paves the way to the solution. It is the pinnacle of the creative problem solving process.

## Creative Problem Solving

The "sudden illumination" (Davis & Hersch, 1980) in which, as if from nowhere, ideas or solutions come to us is a sensation familiar to many of us. In that "magical moment" (Barnes, 2000) we are struck not only with a sense of certainty (Fischbein, 1987) and clarity of understanding (Polya, 1965/1981) but also with a feeling of bliss (Rota, 1997). We remember these moments, and we accept them as a very real and powerful part of our thinking and learning experience. They resonate with the experiences of brilliant thinkers (see, for example, Poincaré, below) and artists (see, for example, Coleridge, below) as we read in their anecdotal accounts a recurring story, a story of suddenness, clarity, lack of conscious effort, and euphoria.

> At the moment when I put my foot on the step, the idea came to me, without anything in my former thought seeming to have paved the way for it . . . I did not verify the idea . . . but I felt a perfect certainty. (Henri Poincaré, cited in Hadamard, 1954, p. 13)

> [I]f that indeed can be called composition in which the images rose up before him as things with parallel production of the correspondent expressions, without any sensation or consciousness of effort. (Coleridge, on the writing of Kubla Kahn, 1816, p. 2)

But this is just the pinnacle of the phenomenon. Although the creative problem-solving process is marked by the suddenness of acquired clarity, it is actually made up of four stages stretched out over time—initiation, incubation, illumination, and verification (Hadamard, 1954)—of which the moment of illumination is but one part.

In the context of solving a mathematical problem, the initiation phase is the deliberate and conscious engagement of the problem. During this stage the solver engages the problem through a process of design. This is an important element in the process in that it creates the tension of unresolved effort that sets up the emotional release at the moment of illumination. The solver, unable to come to a solution, then enters into an incubation phase in which work at the conscious level stops (Dewey, 1933). It is widely believed, and I will take it as given, that the problem continues to be worked on at an unconscious level (Poincaré, 1952). After a varied period of incubation, a rapid coming to mind of the solution, referred to as illumination, accompanies feelings of certainty and other positive emotions. What brings the idea forward to consciousness is unclear. There are theories on aesthetic qualities of the idea (Poincaré, 1952; Sinclair, 2002), effective surprise/shock of recognition (Brunner, 1964), fluency of processing (Whittlesea & Williams, 2001), allowing the brain to rest (Helmholtz, cited in Krutetskii, 1976), or breaking functional fixedness (Maire, cited in Ashcraft, 1989), none of which I will expand on here. The illumination is immediately followed by a verification stage, which is more an examination of the idea/solution that appeared to the mind of the solver as a check for correctness. However, a check for correctness is certainly warranted. Although an illumination is accompanied by a feeling of certainty it is often the case that upon closer examination the solution is shown to be incorrect.

The process of creative problem solving, in general, and the phenomenon of illumination, in particular, are not "part of the theories of logical forms" (Dewey, 1938, p. 103) that we normally associate with mathematical thought. In fact, they are quite the opposite. Unlike the method of problem solving by design described above, creative problem solving is a transcendental and unobservable phenomenon. It lies outside of logic, and as such, it is inextricably linked to another such process, the intuition.

At a very rudimentary level intuition can be thought of as a "hunch" (Bruner, 1964). However, closer examination of intuition shows that its use is, in fact, functionally dependent (Beth & Piaget, 1966; Fischbein, 1987); the context is important. In the process of problem solving, for example, intuition may give you a direction in which to look. In the context of assessing the plausibility of a solution, the intuition can be used in an evaluative form. Fischbein (1987) recognizes the functional dependency of intuition and classifies it according to its role. He refers to a case of a hint of where to look as (inferential) affirmatory intuition and further differentiates these as ground and individual intuitions. Fischbein identifies rapid evaluation as a case of conjectural intuition and claims that it is caused by an expert's ability to consider nonsalient features (including aesthetic elements) of the situation at an unconscious level. There is also a third and a fourth type of intuition that he calls anticipatory and conclusive intuitions. He groups these together as problem-solving intuitions whose characteristic is no different from that of illumination.

Before I continue with a discussion of the imagination, however, it should be noted that the literature treats these aforementioned phenomena—creative problem solving, illumination, and intuition—along with the phenomena of imagination, insight, and aesthetics with little consistency of meaning. They are often used haphazardly (and interchangeably) without definition to talk about situations that fall outside logical reasoning. Together they make up what is sometimes referred to as the extralogical processes of mathematics and, depending on the context in which they are used, can be given varying degrees of credence. In those few cases in which they are defined, the collective literature produces a set of contradictory and overlapping understandings of the individual phenomena. I have, therefore, attempted to provide a set of working definitions, culled from the literature, that I feel will allow me to discuss the role of the imagination in mathematical problem solving in a way that is complimentary and meaningful.

## THE ROLE OF THE IMAGINATION IN PROBLEM SOLVING

Before I engage in such a discussion, however, I need to address something that until now I have simply glossed over, namely, the contradiction between how mathematics is created and how mathematics is represented. As described in the previous section, mathematics often has its roots in the fires of creativity, being born of the extralogical processes of illumination and intuition. However, once created it is "encoded in a linear textual format born out of the logical formalist practice that now dominates mathematics" (Borwein & Jörgenson, 2001). This protocol for the presentation of new mathematics has not only succeeded in distorting the artifacts of mathematics; it has also constructed a false understanding of what it means to "do" mathematics. Certainly, there are instances in which logical deductive reasoning is sufficient to bring about the formation of new mathematics, and in such instances "doing" mathematics can be classified as logical and deductive. However, as described in the section on creative problem solving, such logical and deductive reasoning is not always sufficient. In such instances a greater reliance on the extralogical processes is required to make progress on the problem or to forge new mathematics. To say that "doing" mathematics is always logical and deductive, therefore, is far from accurate. However, knowing that such thinking exists helps us to understand the negative role that the imagination is sometimes seen to play in mathematics.

Reasoning is the currency in which mathematics is traded. It, alone, is responsible for lifting mathematics to the heights of unquestioned certainty. Reconciling this highly structured view of mathematics with the somewhat less structured ideals of the imagination is a difficult task.

> Reasoning indeed depends crucially on imagining, but good reasoning requires the artful handling of imagination, which can as easily divert as support the course of reasoning if left to run its course willy-nilly. (Perkins, 1985, p.14)

However, such thinking most likely results from an impoverished understanding of the imagination, an understanding mired in an association with childhood whimsy. A more informed understanding of the imagination would consist of seeing it as reaching out from where you are (Greene, 2000) along lines of conceivable trajectories as determined by your own experiences (Dewey, 1933; Whitehead, 1959).

On the surface this may seem to be no different from problem solving by design. They both rely heavily on a repertoire of experiences to help them advance the problem. There are two main differences, however. The first is what is meant by experiences. In the case of design a personal relevant experience refers to an actual similar situation that the solver has experienced. In the case of imagination, by contrast, the experience need not be real or relevant, just conceivable. The second characteristic that distinguishes imagination from design lies in the mechanism by which plausibility is evaluated. In problem solving by design, feasibility is evaluated at the conscious level, while in imagination it is evaluated at the unconscious level (Bruner, 1964)—relying on the process of conjectural intuition. As such, "imagination has the pragmatic value that it leaps ahead of the slow-moving caravan of well ordered thoughts and often scouts out reality long before its ponderous master" (Kasner & Newman, 1940).

However, it need not be the passive act of letting the imagination carry your thoughts away on a whimsical (willy-nilly) sojourn, as characterized above. Mathematicians exercise a great deal of control over their imagination, often using it to look out across the mathematical landscape (Burton, 1999). This landscape can be traversed along familiar paths or explored along unfamiliar ones. They imagine where they should go next and what might be there. This is demonstrated in the words of Enrico Bombieri, a well-respected mathematician:

> I would say that my attitude towards mathematics is more that of a problem solver than of a builder of theories. I can paraphrase this by saying that I am not an architect or urban planner, rather more of a painter working on small paintings depicting what the inspiration leads him to. My approach to research consists in looking to the mathematical landscape, taking notice of the things I like and judge interesting and of those I don't care about, and then trying to imagine what should be next. If you see a bridge across a river, you try to imagine what lies on the other shore. If you see a mountain pass between two high mountains, you try to imagine what is in the valley you don't see yet but secretly know must be there. Thus the first step of discovery consists for me in selecting an area of interest and good problems. How does one decide what is interesting? Usually, this is an instinctive process that takes very little time. (quoted in Liljedahl, 2004, p. 122)

However, simply imagining it does not make it so. Realization of the imaginings is required before anything of substance has been created, as Igor Stravinsky (cited in Root-Bernstein & Root-Bernstein, 1999) so eloquently points out:

> Invention presupposes and should not be confused with it. For the act of invention implies the necessity of a lucky find and of achieving full realization of this find. What we imagine does not necessarily take on a concrete form and may remain in a state of virtuality, whereas invention is not conceivable apart from its actually being worked out. Thus, what concerns us here is not imagination in itself, but rather creative imagination: the faculty that helps us pass from the level of conception to the level of realization. (p. x)

The imagination is but a part of the creative process, but it is an important part, a necessary part. It is by the imagination that new ideas are created, and by which new ideas are explored. Whether an idea, or direction of attack, comes through the mystery of the extralogical processes or the rationality of logical processes, its feasibility needs to be evaluated. The act of evaluation, as in problem solving by design, can be done in the form of a thought experiment—"imagine what would happen if . . . "—to follow the thought through to its conclusion along lines of logical inferences (Barbeau, 1985). This applies to both problem solving by design and creative problem solving, and in some cases it is the only form of reason available to us.

When mathematics gets so abstract that physical models and metaphoric understanding become useless, all that remains is the imagination. To be able to envision how things can be in such circumstances is an invaluable tool. To see how things can be "otherwise" is even more valuable. Maxine Greene (2000) defines the imagination as the ability to see that things can be other than as they are. In mathematics, the creation of non-Euclidean geometry is an excellent example of this. Although it could be said that an alternate, yet complete and wholly consistent geometry is an example of something "other than as it is," it is the emergence of the idea that is more an example of imagination. It was mathematicians questioning the need for Euclid's fifth postulate in the framework of Euclidean geometry that started the process. They had the ability to question the status quo of a long established *element* of mathematics, to dare to imagine things as other than what they are. This method of questioning—asking what if, or what if not—is the basis of a form of mathematical inquiry referred to as problem posing (Brown & Walter, 1983). The principal of this form of inquiry is to use systematic and structured questioning to gain insight into a level of sincere inquiry. That is, it is hoped that through adherence to the ideas of problem posing, the students will hit upon a question that they will become sincerely engaged in. The imagination is invoked in a systematic way to formulate new and interesting ideas worthy of mathematical pursuit.

A final consideration of the role of the imagination in problem solving lies in the way in which we engage in the act of creative problem solving. It could be said that every problem has its own language, a language dependent on the specifics of the problem. This language manifests itself in the formal notation and symbols that are created to represent the particulars of the problem. However, it also manifests itself in the less formal discussions of the problem between colleagues. In the absence of colleagues, this discussion may turn to what is often described as self-talk. The problem is, that self-talk exists within the private sanctity of one's own thoughts. It is only in the sharing of them that we can begin to see what occurs in this private dialogue. However, for reasons described above, sincere accounts of self-talk are hard to come by; mathematicians are too well trained in the discourse of deductive logic to be able to speak honestly of their inductive thinking. In fact, in all my research of the literature on creative problem solving I have come across only one account that I would classify as sincere. In it we can see how the imagination and the self-talk intertwine and complement each other.

## IMAGINATION AND SELF-TALK:
## THE CASE OF DOUGLAS R. HOFSTADTER

Douglas R. Hofstadter is not a professional mathematician. He is a college professor of cognitive science and computer science and an adjunct professor of history and philosophy of science, philosophy, comparative literature, and psychology. He is best known for his book *Gödel, Escher, Bach: An Eternal Golden Braid* (1980), for which he won both the American Book Award and the Pulitzer Prize. Although Hofstadter is not a professional mathematician he does do mathematics at a very high level and has a particular passion for Euclidean geometry. He also happens to have a long-standing interest in creativity and consciousness, and he has a unique appreciation for tracking his own creative endeavors at the level of detail that is unsurpassed by any other mathematician who has bothered to put his or her thoughts to paper. He has contributed to *Geometry Turned On: Dynamic Software in Learning, Teaching, and Research* (King & Schattschneider, 1996) a chapter, "Discovery and Dissection of a Geometric Gem," in which he tells the story of mathematical invention in amazing detail and clarity.

I will not dissect the entire chapter for several reasons. The first and most obvious is the incredible amount of time and space that that would require. The second is that although there are a number of very interesting passages that speak to the creative process in general, I will focus only on those that contribute directly to my discussion of self-talk and the imagination. Having said that, however, it would be useful for you to understand the general context of his mathematical encounter.

Hofstadter has only recently come to be impassioned with Euclidean geometry; he was never introduced to the Euler line of a triangle. When he did learn about it, two things immediately struck him: the connectivity of seemingly different attributes and the exclusion of the incenter. So he began a journey of trying to find a connection between the Euler line and the incenter. The result was the discovery of an existing line analogous to the Euler line. The symmetry between these lines helped him to formulate his attack and to then create a third line analogous to both these lines. Along the way he found connections not only between the incenter and the Euler line but also to a number of other known and unknown points of significance. For someone unfamiliar with these terms this will undoubtedly all be gibberish. However, the significance of what I am about to say does not lie in the particulars of the mathematical terminology, but in the way Hofstadter speaks of them, and to them.

In the telling of the story from his unique perspectives, Hofstadter adopts three different voices, a trinity of personas that I have called the *narrator*, the *participant*, and the *mathematician*. I point this out because each of these personas contributes to the anecdotal account in a different way. To explain this let me first define the individual roles that they play in the story.

The narrator moves the story along. As such, he often uses language that is rich in temporal phrases: "and then," or "I started." He also fills in details of the nonmathematical variety seemingly for the purpose of providing context and engaging content. The participant is the voice of real time. This persona reveals the emotions and the thoughts that are occurring to Hofstadter as he is experiencing the phenomenon. Finally, the mathematician is the voice that provides the rational and reasoning underpinnings for why the mathematics behind the whole process is not only valid, but also worthy of discussion. The use of the three personas helps to distinguish between analytic and anecdotal reflection, a most fortuitous result. The way this extrapolates into my analysis of the chapter is as follows:

- The imagination, in the broad sense of reaching out and thought experiment, is evident in the persona of the *narrator*.
- The imagination, in the sense of story, is evident in the persona of the *participant*.
- The imagination, in any sense, is completely absent in the persona of the *mathematician*.

Having dealt with the imagination in the sense of reaching out and thought experiment in the previous section, I will not repeat its role here. Instead, my focus will be on the second of these, the imagination of the participant.

Up until now I have not dealt with the imagination in terms of "storying," the creation of a story. This is an idea that is presented in the work of Kieran Egan (1992b) in his framework of imaginative engagement. I won't go into the details of the framework other than to say that it is descriptive as well as prescriptive. In Figure 4.1, I use the framework in its descriptive sense to analyze each of the six passages in which the voice of the participant is heard.

The spontaneous story Hofstadter tells ends here as the voice of the participant disappears from the passage for good. The passage goes on, however, revealing the mathematical discoveries that he makes in the voices of narrator and mathematician. If "storying" is a product of the imagination, and from the passages above it seems to be, then the imagination plays a very active role in the self-talk that is invoked as we engage with the act of problem solving. Hofstadter's participant has clearly shown how this can be so.

Thus far I have discussed the role that the imagination plays in problem solving descriptively. That is, I have identified places in which the imagination exists within some of the normal practices of mathematics. What remains is to discuss the role of the imagination in mathematics prescriptively; ways in which it can be called upon to enhance experiences otherwise devoid of this mechanism of thought. The most obvious of such experiences is the mathematics classroom.

## IMAGINATION IN THE CLASSROOM

It is not too much of a generalization to characterize the typical mathematics classroom as a place devoid of wonder and imagination. For most pupils, "mathematics consists of a collection of facts together with some skills. The facts must be remembered; the skills practiced" (Burton, 1984, p. 9). As a result, the students "who have never had occasion to learn what mathematics is confuse it with arithmetic and consider it a dry and arid science" (Kovaleskaya, quoted in Barbeau, 1985, p. 63). There are many reasons for this—bland teaching, bland textbooks, and bland curricula. There is little room in such a context for mathematical discovery, wonder, and imagination. Given, however, that we are willing to part with the practices of the traditional mathematics classroom, the question still remains: How do we kindle the fire of the imagination in mathematics students?

**Figure 4.1.** Framework of Imaginative Engagement

| The Participant | Commentary |
|---|---|
| *Figure 1 also shows last, but not least, the poor forgotten incenter (1) I, somehow left out of the party. Although I loved the Euler segment, I was deeply puzzled as to why the incenter I had been excluded (2) from it and felt that the incenter surely had to have its own special way of relating (3) to these four points, or else, perhaps, its own coterie of special friends (although which ones they might be, I had no hunch about).* | The incenter (1) is cast as our hero, the "poor forgotten" character who must struggle to reposition himself in the binary opposites of inclusion/exclusion (2) and relating/not relating (3). |
| *This discovery, which I knew must be as old as the hills, was a relief to me, since it somehow put the incenter back in the same league (4) as the points I felt it deserved to be playing (5) with. Even so, it didn't seem to play nearly as "central" (6) a role as I felt it merited, and I was still a bit disturbed by this imbalance (7), almost injustice (8).* | There is momentary success as our hero is included in the same league (4) to play (5) with the other significant points, a metaphor to heighten the importance of this set. Emphasis of the fact that the incenter is one of the centers of a triangle is achieved through word play (6). But alas, our hero has not yet fully repositioned himself in the binary opposites of balance/imbalance (7) and justice/injustice (8). |
| *Browsing through Coolidge's Chapter One (a small book in itself, rich enough to make me feel humble), I came across something that almost took my breath away. There was apparently a second segment (9) that not only was reminiscent of the Euler segment, but in fact was deeply analogous to it.* | A new character is introduced, a new line segment (9) who turns out to be a friend to our hero, the incenter. |
| *And to my great pleasure, it restored the honor (10) of the incenter, while also elevating the Nagel point to a level of respect (11) much higher than I had previously accorded it. I wondered (12) to my self, "Why does this fantastic (13) second segment have no standard name? Why are the two of them not treated by geometers as precisely equal (14) companions?"* | Assigning of transcendent human qualities of honor (10) and respect (11) to the incenter and the Nagel point, respectively. Meanwhile, the wonderful qualities of the new segment are expressed (13), prompting him to wonder (12) why it has been cast on the wrong side of the binary opposites equality/inequality (14). |
| *Surely, I thought, there is something more to it than this. In mathematics, such a striking (15) and intricate (16) analogy can't just happen by accident (17)! There's got to be a reason for it (18).* | The wonderful characteristics of this new segment are continuing to be expressed (15, 16), again prompting him to wonder (18) why it has been cast on the wrong side of the binary opposite of accident/causal (17). |
| *I was baffled. Why was this companion (19) segment—which I began calling the Nagel segment (20), after the discoverer of its outlier endpoint—so neglected (21)? Was it truly less important than the Euler segment (22)? Or was it just that it had been discovered at a time when people were beginning to lose interest in this kind of geometry (23)? I could not help but mull this over, and the image of these two segments, each one lopsidedly cutting the other into two pieces, reverberated through my head intensely.* | The transcendent human qualities of companionship (19) and neglect (21) are superimposed onto this newly named segment (20). Again, the cause of this neglect is pondered (22, 23). |

Consider an example. I bring a bicycle into my classroom and tell the students that this is my new 18-speed Rock Blaster mountain bike (example comes from Norma Presmeg). We explore how it can be that my bike has 18 gears when there are only 3 chain rings and 6 sprockets. We make a diagram and figure out that there are 18 combinations. From this we can make a calculation, for every gear, of how many times the wheel will turn (or how far the bike moves) with one turn of the crank. We realize from this table that there are, in fact, only 16 unique speeds on my bicycle. We can graph some of the relationships in the table to get a nice curve, and maybe make predictions as to what would be other good chain ring and sprocket combinations to have. In the course of a lesson we've managed to cover a lot of mathematics.

Such a lesson would be imaginative, to say the least. However, the imagination lies within the teacher, not the student. Furthermore, given that the very real bike is in front of the students, the likelihood that the imagination is going to be ignited, in the form either of reaching out or thought experiment, is slim. The problem is that, as engaging as such an activity is, we are not *fully* developing a very important aspect of mathematics—abstraction. Sure, we abstracted the bike into a diagram of gears, and then into a table, and then into a graph, all the while keeping the Rock Blaster mountain bike as the object of our focus. This may seem appealing. We're espousing the benefits of situated learning (or historical mathematics, or ethnomathematics, depending on our example). The type of abstraction demonstrated here has a name. Freudenthal, in his work on the Real Mathematics Education Project in the Netherlands, calls it *horizontal mathematization* (Treffers, 1993).

Horizontal mathematization is where the real object (or situation, or story) that the mathematics is built around remains the object of focus during the abstraction process. Freudenthal claims, however, that in mathematics this is not enough to satisfy *all* of what it means to abstract. He proposes that a second dimension be added, called *vertical mathematization*, in which the object of focus be a mathematical object (see Figure 4.2). In our example of the mountain bike this could look like a number of different things. The initial diagram that allowed us to see that there were 18 combinations of chain rings and sprockets could become the object of focus that gets abstracted to a more and more general such diagram, from which would emerge the Fundamental Theorem of Counting. Another option is to abstract the table, or the graph. Even the relationship between the table and the graph could be abstracted toward an understanding of function. Mathematics is like a page of hypertext where even the spaces are hyperlinks; every item (including the spaces) has the potential to become the beginning of a vertical path of investigation.

**Figure 4.2.** Diagram of Mathematical Abstraction

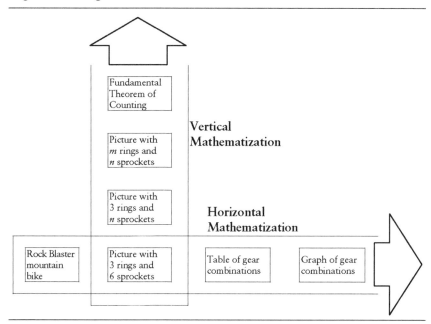

This second, very important dimension of mathematical activity is easily overlooked when frameworks such as situated learning, ethnomathematics, and historical mathematics are implemented. The compelling threads of "reality" that these frameworks use to introduce topics wear thin as they attempt to move in a vertical direction. The temptation to remain attached to the "real" object of focus that was used to introduce the topic is overwhelming. But in doing so the mathematics gets cast in a supporting role. The consequence is that students learn *about* mathematics versus *with* mathematics. More important, the students' imaginations are not activated in the ways that they could, and should, be in order for the mathematics to become engaging. Without the second dimension the mathematics is left in the background and the focus remains on the "real" object of focus. So how do we remedy this?

Let me answer this by presenting yet another example, this time from George Gadanidis. Consider a game that I want to play where I roll two dice. The details of the game are as follows: The dice are rolled one at a time and the goal is to get a sum of eight. Mathematically this game can be developed in a number of different directions. Regardless of which direction it develops in, however, the dice are the real and central object of focus.

The particular direction I will take this in is examining what the second die needs to be, given the first one, in order for the sum to be eight. I can make a table of first die versus second one, where the second die is *dependent* on the outcome of the first. This table is then graphed. So far we've managed to quite effectively create horizontal mathematization through our exploration. Now, what if the sum was to be nine rather than eight? Does this count as vertical mathematization? Because the dice are still the central focus of our engagement the answer is no. However, if we were to set the sum at four it would be.

At first glance this seems not that different from a sum of eight or nine, but when you consider the fact that the dice are rolled one at a time it starts to take on new meaning. Consider what the second die would need to be in order for the sum to be four, given that the first die rolled is a six. The reality of the dice begins to fade as they take on a metaphoric role in development of new mathematical concepts. That second die must be negative two, as can be seen by the patterns in both the tables and the graphs. By replacing the lead role of the real dice with metaphorical dice the mathematics moves into the foreground and the vertical mathematization can begin.

However, in the urgency to attend to the need to abstract there is a temptation to rush, too early, to set a metaphoric role for the object of focus. There is an abundance of such examples in mathematics, usually in the form of word problems. Word problems are written in such a way as to strip them of any of the "reality" of the situation they are meant to represent. As much as these types of problems manage to attend to the need for vertical mathematization, they are all guilty of ignoring the need for horizontal mathematization.

A balance is needed, as it always is, between the use of characters and situations as the real focus of our exploration and the metaphorical support of our exploration. As such, we must weave our explorations carefully, creating situations that can begin as real objects of focus but then effectively give themselves to *metaphors*—without disengaging our students. Herein lies the challenge, for such a feat would succeed in not only invoking the imagination, but also invoking it within the mathematics.


## CONCLUSION

What it means to "do" mathematics is disputable, as is what it means to use your "imagination" in doing mathematics. In this chapter I have attempted to show that regardless of your understandings of these two concepts, they do intersect. The imagination has an indisputable role in the "doing" of mathematics.

*Chapter 5*

# Imagination and the Teaching of Literature: Interpretive and Ethical Implications

## GEOFF MADOC-JONES

At present, English language arts (ELA) teachers are being asked to perform a diverse range of tasks:

- Teach children to read and write and communicate orally, through the enrichment and discipline of the verbal imagination.
- Train students in the language skills necessary for employment and for functioning in society.
- Introduce students to and immerse them in the history of society and of individuals, through narrative.
- Help students develop an in-depth, diverse, and detailed knowledge of human character, principally through the study of literature.
- Encourage students to develop an understanding of certain fundamental philosophical ideas, particularly ethics, through the analysis and discussion of works of literature.
- Provide students the opportunity to become fluent in the use of a variety of poetic and narrative forms and the acquisition of a command of the intricate logic of discourse that language, rhetoric, and grammar codify.
- Lead students to develop cogency, a sense of an individual style and voice, and the organization of thought through writing and rewriting.
- Have students experience and acquire aesthetic understanding through experiencing works of literature as well as through individual creative achievement.
- Immerse students in poetic language as opposed to language as an instrument for technical advancement.

These are but a few of the diverse demands placed on the ELA curriculum, but I would argue that, while all the preceding examples are important, its fundamental goal should be the education of the will, the emotions, and the intellect through a conversation with literature. In this quest the role of the imagination is crucial, for only if a certain quality of imaginative understanding is developed can an individual be attracted to the ideal and the practice of a virtuous and humane life.

The will is a faculty, set of abilities, or dispositions involved in initiating a choice or decision. These acts of willing are sometimes called volitions, which include cognitive, affective, and conative elements. The cognitive consists of thinking, learning, and remembering; the affective of feelings (sensations, emotions, and impressions); and the conative of planning, will power, and intentionality. The conative refers to the fundamental desires and drives of the human psyche.

For those concerned with ethical education the problem is how best to initiate the young into those ways of understanding that will bring about right actions and lay the foundation for the virtuous life. Thus in ethical terms, the debate centers around the problem of free agency and its relation to the origins and conditions of responsible behavior. Oakeshott (1989) sees this freedom as being essential to what it means to be a human being:

> What distinguishes a human being, indeed what constitutes a human being, is not merely his having to think, but his thoughts, his beliefs, doubts, understandings, his awareness of his own ignorance, his wants, preferences, choices, sentiments, emotions, purposes, and his expression of them in utterances or actions which have meanings; and a necessary condition of all or any of this is that he must have *learned* it. The price of the intelligent activity which constitutes being human is learning. (p. 20; italics in the original)

Oakeshott is arguing that because we are not fully determined by nature we have to learn the volitional practices that allow us to make free decisions. The role of education in this regard becomes crucial, as it is no more nor less than the initiation of the young into specific normative forms of intelligent activity.

While this freedom to carry out intelligent activity is influenced by the past, it does not hold sway over it. That is the part that memory plays in our lives. Hannah Arendt (1977) connects memory with the imagination, "Memory, the mind's power of having present what is irrevocably past and thus absent from the senses, has always been the most plausible paradigmatic example of the mind's power to make invisibles present" (p. 11). She then compares the role that "memory" plays in relation to the past with the role that "will" has to the future.

The moment we turn our mind to the future, we are no longer concerned with "objects" but with projects, and it is not decisive whether they are formed spontaneously or as anticipated reactions to future circumstances. . . . In other words we are dealing with matters that never were, that are not yet, and that may never be. (p. 14)

The literature student finds that she sits at the crossroads of the past and the future. The works studied come from the past; they form in some way a canon or are part of a tradition with which she may enter into a dialogue. In education, this dialogue is part of what Oakeshott argues is a conversation that began in the primeval forests and is composed of a diverse set of voices.

The development of imagination as an essential aspect of liberal learning, which is an education in imagination, an initiation into the art of this conversation in which we learn to recognize the voices; to distinguish their different modes of utterance, to acquire the intellectual and moral habits appropriate to this conversational relationship and thus to make our *debut dans la vie humaine*. (p. 39, italics in the original)

However, education is also prospective and looks to the future as well as the past, a future that is in part projected by a willing self that has been influenced, shaped, formed, and directed by the imaginative works of the past. Thus, it is the education of reason, of desire, and of dispositions that form the conditions of the emerging will that should lie at the center of the study of the language arts. Studying the works of the past enriches the memory, but the will must also be tempered in imaginative practices that enable students to express their own projects concerned with tomorrow.

In this chapter I am going to look at aspects of the works of the philosophers Paul Ricoeur and Martha C. Nussbaum, who are most insightful in the attempt to develop a rich concept of the imagination as it relates to the study of literature. From Ricoeur's work the relation between linguistic imagination, metaphor, the positing of possible worlds, and self-understanding will be looked at, while Nussbaum will be used to investigate the role of the study of literature in the developing of ethical understanding and virtue.

## METAPHOR AND LINGUISTIC IMAGINATION

Ricoeur (1997) is critical of rhetorical theories of metaphor that classify it merely as a trope or a figure of speech and that do not give an account of the generative process that accounts for its formation. This is because "the metaphorical process occurs at another level, at the level of the sentence and of discourse as a whole" (p. 131), and not at the level of the word.

Ricoeur argues that as one moves from description to interpretation, "the imagination is considered less in terms of 'vision' than in terms of 'language.' Or to put it more exactly, imagination is assessed as an indispensable agent in the creation of meaning in and through language" (quoted in Kemp & Rasmussen, 1989, p. 1). Ricoeur emphasizes the linguistic functioning of imagination, where there exists "not just epistemological and political imagination, but also, and more fundamentally, a linguistic imagination which generates and regenerates meaning through the living power of metaphoricity" (p. 14). He affirms the poetical role of imagining—that is, its ability to say one thing in terms of another, or to say several things at the same time, thereby creating new meaning. This he calls "semantic innovation" and it gains its importance from the fact that the productive unit of metaphor is not the word but the sentence. This power of imagination to transform given meanings into new ones enables us to see the future as an opening up of possibilities. "We have thought too much in terms of a will which submits and not enough of an imagination which opens up" (quoted in Kemp & Rasmussen, 1989, p. 4). Ricoeur thus claims that the productive power of imagination is not primarily visual but verbal, which means that if images emerge as spoken before being seen they can no longer be reduced to quasi-material residues of sensual perception (that is, objects for merely empirical study) or modifications or negations of direct perceptions (that is, eidetic phenomenology). Thus if the image exists in a verbal dimension prior to becoming the focus of perception, then linguistic imagination is originary and is a productive force while the nonverbal is reproductive.

At the heart of the linguistic imagination is the verbal metaphor where figurative meaning emerges in the interplay between identity and difference. This meeting place of two semantic fields, the literal and the figurative, is where the action of metaphoricity brings different meanings into a state of identity. That which was predicatively impertinent at a literal level becomes predicatively pertinent at a new level, namely, the poetic. For example; take the statement, "The life of ignorance is a dark cave." We have here a dissimilarity, a state of semantic shock, and because the predicate does not follow literally from the expectations set up by the subject, it seems initially impertinent. There is a moment of rupture in the semantic field, because we know that ignorance" is not "a dark cave" at the literal level. The issue then becomes, how are they to be reconciled so as to produce a new meaning? This takes place through the imagination working as the generative power of language, so the "cave" is *seen as* "ignorance," but only after its semantically impertinent state has been realized. Thus imagination is the act of responding to the pressure for new meanings that life throws at us because we are future-facing beings; we live formed by the past but also always look to the future.

But the imagination needs images; otherwise it would remain invisible, and the visual image is the moment when the verbal turns sensible. Perhaps the idea of "seeing-as" is the key to the sensual aspect of poetic imagination, where sense and image are held together in an intuitive manner, so that from the quasi-sensory mass of tacit imagery a semantic order is formed by imagination, which also has the capacity to move back from intuition to conceptual meaning. These two ways of moving, from the intuitive to the conceptual and back again, form a creative tension between expression and interpretation that can be helpful in the ELA classroom.

> The seeing-as activated in reading ensures the joining of meaning with imagistic fullness, (and) that conjunction is no longer something outside language since it can be reflected as a relationship. Seeing-as contains a ground, a foundation, this is precisely, a resemblance. It is a schema which unites the empty concept with the blind impression. . . . Thanks to its character as half thought and half experience, it joins the light of sense with the fullness of the image. In this way, the non-verbal and the verbal are firmly united at the core of the image-ing function of language. (Ricoeur, 1989, pp. 199–200)

The function of imagination in poetry or myth is defined by Ricoeur as the "disclosure of unprecedented worlds, an opening onto possible worlds which transcend the limits of our actual world" (Kemp & Rasmussen, 1989, pp. 5–6). This approach to imagination thus differs from a structural or existentialist one in its concentration on the capacity of world-disclosure yielded by texts. In short, interpretation is not "confined to the objective analysis of texts, nor to the subjective existential analysis of the authors of texts; its primary concern is with the worlds which these authors and texts open up" (pp. 5–6).

This opening up of possible worlds by the imagination assists in our understanding of how we exist in the world with others. First, we cannot come to know ourselves through any direct path but only through the detour of interpreting signs and works and by the deciphering of the products of the imagination in myths, dreams and symbols; "the shortest route from the self to itself is through the images of others" (Kemp & Rasmussen, 1989, pp. 5–6). Second, the imagination is not confined to the circle of interpretation. The projection of possible worlds through semantic innovation is an essential ingredient of the dynamism of ethical action. Semantic innovation points toward the possible transformation of the social world because of the freedom inherent in projecting possible worlds; there is "no action without imagination" (p. 6). What is interpreted in a text is the proposing of a world that I might inhabit and into which I can project my own desires. Thus the world is the whole set of references opened by every sort of descriptive or poetic texts I have read, interpreted, and loved. To understand these texts is to interpolate among the predicates of our situation all those meanings that, from a simple environment (*Umwelt*), make a world (*Welt*). Indeed we owe a large part of the enlarging of our horizon of existence to poetic works. (Ricoeur, p. 80)

As ELA teachers we are most interested in the recovery of the capacity of language to create and re-create, to discover reality in the process of being created. Language in the making celebrates reality in the making. Literal meaning is shattered as metaphor is formed, and as language is re-created and increased our sense of reality is likewise, so that in metaphor we experience the metamorphosis of both language and reality.

As well as its role in the creation of new meaning through metaphor and thereby opening up the possibility of a new reality, the poetic form instantiates three referential functions at once, which are of import to the language arts. There is first-order reference, the immediate world of perception (empirical reality), the author's and the reader's, as contained in the ordinary literal meaning; there is then second-order reference, a world where the meaning contained in the metaphor is possible. The first-order reference is suspended while the semantic innovation plays its role, whose purpose is to disclose new ways of being in the world; therefore, in its most fundamental sense it is an ontological event. Thus linguistic imagination is committed to the role of both semantic and ontological innovation. The third-order reference comes from the idea that language in its poetic form also refers to itself. I include it in this analysis because it has an important pedagogic role to play in the ELA classroom, as the teacher may use it to highlight students' realization of the structured nature of their own thoughts.

Thus literature has the capacity to perform these functions in a way that other linguistic modes do not: It can sweep back to the being that is revealed and leap forward to the language that is revealing both itself and a world. However, language does not merely refer to the world; it also has the capacity to form a world by opening up new horizons of meaning for the speaker; the writer; and equally important, the reader. The linguistic imagination liberates the reader into a space of possibility, suspending the reference to the immediate world of perception, both the author's and the reader's, thereby disclosing new ways of being in the world.

The innovative power of linguistic imagination is not some decorative excess or effusion of subjectivity, but the capacity of language to open up new worlds. The function of imagination in poetry and myth is to disclose unprecedented worlds and create openings onto possible worlds that transcend the limit of the actual world.

Metaphor epitomizes this process by creating new connections rather than mere congruence and by making a similarity out of what was previously dissimilar. The degree of "semantic impertinence" of the dissimilar elements is related to any gains in new meaning. Clichés are old metaphors that once created a new pertinence but no longer do so. These are then available for renewal through a new metaphoric relation where the "is like" element and the "is not" element are intrinsically connected. This is the way in which language deals with the indeterminacy of the future and enables the speaker or writer to create new meaning. This is the creative imagination at work poetically and represents one of the most important aspects of language arts education. Children who are schooled in metaphoric thought learn to become semantically impertinent thinkers who are not just capable of producing an apt metaphor for a verse-writing exercise but who have as a constitutive feature of their thought the capacity to think what is not the case. This connection between seeing that which is not the case and educating the imagination show that these elements are not merely the frills acquired in the literary classroom but are essential components of being able to make sense of a world that is both finite and indeterminate. According to Ricoeur (1977), a metaphor is a rhetorical process to liberate the capacity of a fiction to redescribe the reality.

Ricoeur's emphasis on semantic innovation, on creativity in language, on how metaphor makes new meaning by challenging our sense of similarity and difference, for example, or how narratives structure time in variable, changing, and novel ways, makes him an essential authority who cannot be ignored in the field of language arts theory. Ricoeur is also interested in how individual speakers (artists, poets, novelists, but also ordinary folks) can do new things with existing materials and collective instruments for signification, even perhaps transforming the code in the process.

Throughout his theory of hermeneutics, and in particular in his work on metaphor and narrative, Ricoeur shows that the meaning-making powers of consciousness are nothing by themselves but depend always on language. He stresses the general status of self-understanding by incorporating the mediation of symbols and myths into reflection as a part of the history of culture, and rejects a self-consciousness that would be immediate, direct, and transparent to itself, and shows instead the necessity of a detour by the signs and the works of the cultural world.

In his later work Paul Ricoeur defines his goal as the "step-by-step approximations of a solution to a single problem, that of understanding language at the level of productions such as poems, narratives, and essays, whether literary or philosophical" (1976, p. xi). At the heart of his investigations is the question "What is the meaning of being?" that is, What is the meaning of being human? (Ricoeur, 1984, p. 64). This first question, according to Ricoeur, subsumes "questions of methodology to the reign of primordial ontology," so that prior to or concurrently with epistemic questions another question must also be considered: "Instead of asking, how do we know? It will be asked, what is the mode of being of that being who exists only in understanding?" (p. xi). If we as human beings have a being that exists only in understanding and if understanding emerges through language, and if such understandings are not natural but require participation by each individual in a historically formed culture, then education should be primarily concerned with the development of understanding. Ricoeur (1991) claims that "there is no real understanding that is not mediated by signs, symbols and texts; [and] in the last resort understanding coincides with the interpretation given to these mediating terms" (p. 15). This argues for a special place for the study of language at the heart of the educational enterprise. Furthermore, if understanding emerges primarily as a result of the interpretation of the mediating forms, then hermeneutics has a key role to play not only in theory in education but also in practical issues of pedagogy. In particular it renders questionable for education any theory that sees the psychology of learning as having to do with generic entities that exist separate from mediation by culture and its interpretive practices.

## TEXT AND READER

What must be considered is whether interpretation is seen as a subjective act *on* the text or is an "objective process of interpretation which would be the act *of* the text" (Ricoeur, 1991, p. 61). For language arts teachers this is a key pedagogic issue, because if the act is one done *by* the subject on the text, then the reader, even with the restraint of syntactic structure serving as a coding model for higher functions, has priority and his intentions and lived experience are primary. When this is the case teachers are interested in encouraging students to check their inner mental states as they appropriate the text by constructing meaning out of it. Questions often attempt to elicit reports of the students' responses to the text, such as, What do you think of the text? How does it make you feel? Do you have an opinion? It is not that these types of questions are necessarily inappropriate; it is just that they are not the primary ones in any program that seeks to teach pupils how to understand texts hermeneutically.

Educationally, what needs to be asked concerning how a student understands a literary text, *The Cherry Orchard*, for example, is not what she thinks of the play but, once she knows the play well enough, how she is potentially changed by experiencing Chekhov's work. Its mode of being exists for the purpose of doing its work on the reader or, if performed, the audience, as Shaw always claimed concerning his plays and their prefaces. The reader's responsibility is to learn how to approach the work and not to introduce uninformed opinions that will only get in the way of the possibility of its truth emerging. This does not mean that the reader is passive; in fact, only the giving up of premature and uninformed opinion formation can enable the possibility of an authentic experience through performance to emerge.

Ricoeur (1991) argues that if the text seeks to place us in its meaning then to interpret is to "follow the thought opened up by the text, to place oneself en route towards the orient of the text" (p. 61). The reader of the text "appropriates" it, by which Ricoeur means that interpretation culminates in the self-interpretation of the subject "who henceforth understands himself better, understands himself differently, or simply begins to understand himself" (p. 57). Self-understanding, however, will always be mediated in part by a conversation with the cultural tradition in which the self documents and mirrors itself. Ricoeur emphasizes the relationship between interpretation and reflection, but reminds us that

> reflection is nothing without the mediation of signs and works, and that explanation is nothing if it is not incorporated as an intermediary stage in the process of self-understanding. In short, hermeneutical reflection—or reflective hermeneutics—the constitution of the *self* is contemporaneous with the constitution of *meaning*. (p. 57)

If one of the roles of language arts is to assist students in coming to a more authentic self-understanding, then the question of their own temporality in a world of action and suffering must be investigated. Ricoeur is concerned to show that the reading of literature is part of an activity that is, in my opinion, at the heart of a language arts education. This is the coming to a deeper and richer understanding of the self, not just for its own sake, but so that this experience of the self in a world of action can lead to a new understanding of that world. Becoming educated demands a particular response to the epistemological, conceptual, aesthetic, and moral questions posed by the world of action; these questions constitute the subtext of the curriculum, and the student response to a work is formed through an appropriative engagement with the cultural heritage for the purpose of redescribing the world as an experience of the self.

Ricoeur (1991) sees the study of literature as directed to the examination of the text as a reconstituted reality that takes into account historical considerations but is grounded in the phenomenon of the reader's appropriation.

Perhaps it is at this level of self-understanding that the mediation effected by the text can best be understood. In contrast to the tradition of the *cogito* and to the pretension of the subject to know itself by immediate intuition, it must be said that we understand ourselves only by the long detour of the signs of humanity deposited in cultural works. What would we know of love and hate, of moral feelings and, in general, of all that we call *the self*, if these had not been brought to language and articulated by literature? Thus what seems most contrary to subjectivity and what structural analysis discloses as the structure of the text, is the very medium within which we can understand ourselves. (p. 143)

Ricoeur has given language arts teachers a compelling theoretical basis for the teaching of literature and has also provided strong principles on which a humanistic pedagogy of reading can be based. A pedagogy that neither falls into the scientist nor the subjectivist camps, but which provides a hermeneutic practice that will enable students to study texts both structurally and semantically while understanding themselves better.

This understanding of the self through the study of literature and the development of the linguistic imagination form a basis for arguing that an important role for the ELA is the development of ethical understanding.

## LITERATURE AND ETHICAL EDUCATION

Martha C. Nussbaum (1990) has also argued for a view of literature that is not merely based on a formalist, textual, or aesthetic approach but that incorporates philosophical, and in particular ethical, theories in its interpretation. This literary-philosophical approach has in her view a number of important benefits both for literary studies and for philosophy, and a key element in this marriage is her stress on the importance of the emotions, not only for an understanding and appreciation of literature but also in ethical discourse. The conventional view is that philosophy is based on reason and literature is based on the emotions. She contends that because of this dichotomy philosophy has become lifeless and its prose technical and literary studies have become too immersed in formal and textual analysis, which has lacked the analytical tools to connect literary works with important philosophical theory.

A key element in her theory is the important role that feelings play both in literary studies and in ethics. She talks about the epistemology of feeling and argues against the traditional hostility that many philosophers have had concerning feelings. Feelings have been seen as unnecessary, unreliable, inexact, or potentially dangerous for the kind of detached rational thought that lies at the heart of philosophy. Nussbaum (1990) points out that often feelings are more reliable than beliefs and that there is a most important role for feelings in the development of ethical understandings. We are not detached from the world and often sense our outrage toward or support of an action prior to or at the same time as our cognitions. To paraphrase Aristotle, to be rational about everything is to be irrational. Do we need reason to tell us we are in love?

However, Nussbaum does not see feelings as some vague, fuzzy, romantic notion that provides a warm context for thought, but as an integral part of the priority of the particular and sensitive perception, both of which are key elements in ethical reasoning. Her contention is that general ethical prescriptions cannot in themselves tell people what their ethical reaction should be to any particular issue with which they are faced. These generalities can only be of use once the particularities of a situation have been perceived. Without a sensitive and intense attention to the particulars, to the nuances and details of the situation at hand, the application of some rationally developed general tenet can be dangerous. The development of this sensitive perception of the particular cannot take place merely by studying philosophy, because by its logic philosophy has an interest in the generality, and while often examples are given to illustrate points in philosophic argument, they do not have sufficient richness, depth, and detail. Furthermore, they are written in a style that does not encourage linguistic sensitivity.

Nussbaum argues that only in literature, and in particular in certain novels, can we find situations described in such detail, with such attention to linguistic complexity, with such emphasis on the unique and particular nature of human experience can we find the appropriate expression of the reality of the human condition that is the purpose of ethics to explain. It is not, in her view, a simple question of the application of reasoned judgments; there is a required and necessarily prior attention to feelings that have been aroused by perceptions of the particular.

Thus Nussbaum sees an important role for feelings in any attempt to interpret the ethical component of a literary work. But this is not sufficient, for what is also needed is a thorough knowledge of general claims that philosophy makes, because without them it is not possible to interpret the meaning of the perceptions experienced. It is not that reason has no role to play in literary studies; in fact, Nussbaum would claim that we need reasoned feelings and felt reason. Both are necessary individually but only sufficient together.

Nussbaum's ideas have serious implications for both the teaching of literature and the study of literature. Literature being taught in a manner that does not take into account the relation between feelings, reason, and ethics is being taught in a seriously deficient manner. Great literature is a most important source for the gaining of understanding about the human condition in general and the particular existential state of the reader. As well as all the other benefits and pleasure to be derived from the study of literature the development of ethical sensitivity and becoming literate in moral discourse must be seen by teachers as fundamental goals of their teaching. When studying the teaching of literature, this ethical component must be seen as a key element in any educationally defensible practice. This means that not only must the teacher be aware of the potential for moral development for students that is inherent in the reading of good literature; they must also actively teach in a way in which the classroom discourse reflects the sensitivity and complexity of the text. In fact the teacher will better find the way to teach the novel from the novel itself than from some theory of instruction or learning. The curriculum and the instructional approach are to be found in the works themselves. It also follows from this that no methodology for the studying or the teaching of literature can stray too far from the nature of literature itself.

The role that the study of literature plays in the development of moral virtue is a most important one, in the following ways. First, it is necessary to conceive of what is meant by moral virtue. The view I am proposing is one that sees moral virtues as those faculties that must exist in the human soul in order for the question "How do I lead the good life?" to be coherent. These are the human goods to which anyone would aspire who seriously asked that question. They are not reducible to one overriding good, but are many and incommensurable, even if linked, and neither are they merely to be attained by rigid obedience to duty or obligation. They cannot be conceived of as being merely the attributes of a detached and atomistic individual living outside a community, a tradition, or a framework of worth. They refer, however, not only to social obligations but also to the development of a certain kind of self, one that values him- or herself and sees that there is a strong, necessary connection between virtue and happiness.

Second, it is important to note that any moral theory dominated by a notion that the role of reason is merely to restrain dangerous feelings and desires has little place for the emotions. The moral life may be regarded as one either of attending to and fulfilling contractual obligations that it is in my interest to keep or the avoidance of sin, because of the dangers of retribution, or of keeping a balance or mean between all the conflicting desires that inhabit my soul. When it is seen in this way reason is often regarded as the governor that restrains the inappropriate desire or feeling; it is reason that saves us from being merely a slave to our passions. This is particularly the case when dealing with self-regarding virtues, those that have to do primarily with one's own character, such as temperance and prudence, where reason assists in the avoidance, suppression, and denial of gluttony or profligate behavior. We must not downplay the importance of reason in the control of these potentially dangerous emotional states, but a moral theory merely based on obligation, where the emotions are seen as dangerous, does not deal with an important, more positive area of moral life. These contain the desires that epitomize the aspirations of individuals to work with and for their communities for the creation of a better life. In regard to these aspirational virtues, such as justice, empathy, and truth telling, there is no need for reason to restrain the related emotion or to suppress inappropriate ones. The role of reason is to guide and assist in the flourishing and development of such desires. The wish to live well with and for others is as important in the development of virtue as is the reasoned attention to duty.

The study of literature can be of great value in the development of both self-regarding virtues as well as those that deal with our relationship with the other. In regard to the self, the study of literature can provide the student with the complex, unique concrete particulars that provide a more real context for moral decision making. Furthermore, the linguistic imagination, "seeing as," is a key component in this process. Philosophy deals with generalities, but what is also needed for the developing child are rich examples of human experience that reflect more truly the messy and contingent nature of moral decision making. Often moral disagreements do not exist at the general or abstract level. For example, during the recent Gulf War, both staunch supporters and opponents of the war would have agreed that courage was a virtue that they both admired, but what help was this for the young soldier faced with the realities of combat? It requires courage to go to Iraq and courage to resist; what is of importance is how and why individual decisions are taken. It would be beneficial for students to study a work of literature dealing with the complexities and difficulties of these decisions, because in this way they would develop the sensitive, imaginative perceptions that are the necessary preconditions for competent moral discourse.

It is in the development of these complex and nuanced perceptions, particularly in relation to the aspirational virtues, that the importance of the study of literature lies. It is not a fail-safe method of producing ethical people; however, without something of this kind, particularly in today's world, with the virtual collapse of traditional value systems and the growth of a pluralistic society, the capacity of young people to create an ethic of authenticity will be much more difficult.

## CONCLUSION

It should be emphasized that this approach to the teaching of literature is not one based merely on a detached technique, but in fact is an aspect of all forms of dialogue, that is, the dialectic of language and experience. Students must be prepared to move beyond the limitations of their subjective responses in order to imaginatively be a part of the meaning of the literary text. This means that the related procedures of analysis and interpretation must be joined in an imaginative way if the student is to attain a full understanding of the literary reading experience.

The teacher's goal is to assist the student in becoming an active participant in such interpretive, imaginative readings. Literary texts represent one of the most educationally important ways of coming to understand the self and the world. The educative study of literature must base its practice on the idea that the text and the world are connected.

A literary text is one that provides an imaginative rendering of reality, and as such its interpretation requires a more complex series of moves than do other, more informational kinds of texts. The literary text emerges from a background that does not form part of a series of verifiable sources as in science, history and philosophy. The literary author re-forms these sources into a text filtered through figurative language, literary conventions, and cultural and social values. Thus the author's message is not transmitted directly to the reader, who, to understand its meaning, will need to have the imaginative capacity necessary for interpretation to take place. Furthermore, the student will also need to become aware of her own reception of the work and to place it not only within the context of her own reading history but within the reading tradition in which she lives.

All of the above must be taken into account when teaching students to become capable interpretive readers of literary texts. The teacher must be able to provide the kind of practical advice that makes that possible. This task is complex, the achievement difficult, but the rewards are great. To reiterate what I said at the beginning of the chapter: The goal is the education of the will, the emotions, and the intellect through a conversation with literature. The chapter has shown part of the way in which imagination is crucial in the forming of people who are attracted to the ideal and the practice of a virtuous and humane life.

*Chapter 6*

# Imaginative Science Education:
# Two Problems and a
# Possible Solution

## SEAN BLENKINSOP

Several years ago, while I was just finishing my graduate work, there was a seemingly minor discovery that led to a profound concern. The discovery was made by several science education professors who found that, after having spent convocation wandering around doing interviews with new graduates, a surprising number of the graduates had little or no understanding of some of the most basic concepts of science. Many of the students gave responses that for science professors smacked of "prescientific" fantasy. For example—and this one really seemed to capture everyone's attention—when asked about where the "stuff," the matter, comes from that allows a tiny acorn to turn, over time, into a massive oak tree, the vast majority of students confidently answered, with little hesitation, that it came from the earth. Gasp! Now the part that made this story into an international concern and not just one that a few gray-haired professors worried over was that the graduates were, for the most part, newly minted science graduates at Harvard University. Before going any further, I am guessing that those of you who know the "correct" answer are now raving about the quality of education at such a reputable institution; however, some of you may be Harvard grads and are still wondering where all that mass might come from, if not from the earth. The answer is it comes from the air. Remember all those science classes where you learned about photosynthesis; plants taking up carbon dioxide and giving off oxygen; and, if you were lucky, the Krebs citric acid cycle? Well, in all that stuff was the basic piece of information that he oak is yanking molecules of carbon dioxide out of the molecule-filled air and stripping off the carbon, which it then uses as the fundamental building block for the organic life that it is. Now, a single molecule of carbon isn't very big or heavy, but strip billions of them from the air, organize them, hold them together, and you get quite a structure.

The Harvard science educators seemed to think that this whole problem was an indication of how poor the scientific literacy of the American people was and how hard it is to dislodge cultural "folk knowledge" even in the light of good solid scientific evidence. I am not sure this is the whole story, especially in light of the fact that many of you who didn't think you knew the answer, or had the wrong answer, are now banging your heads, muttering, "I knew that, I knew the tree was mostly carbon and therefore air, I just forgot." My proposition, which I will spend a bit of time arguing in support of, is that the problem lies with two different educational beliefs taken together that have been de rigueur in public schooling in North America for more than 50 years. I am going to call these two problems the *child-centered empirical evidence fallacy* and the *concrete versus abstract conundrum*, respectively, and lay them at the feet of what is commonly referred to as progressive education. Now before you decide that I am about to leap into a traditionalist diatribe on standards, Truth, and teacher-centered knowledge, please hear me out, because that is not the move I will make. First, because that progressive/traditional dualism is not particularly helpful and, second, because there is another option that helps children to make better scientific sense of their world and avoid looking like knuckleheads on their college graduation day. This other option is imaginative education.

## TWO PROBLEMS FOR SCIENTIFIC LITERACY

### The Child-Centered Empirical Evidence Fallacy

There is a story told about philosopher Ludwig Wittgenstein in which he accosts several students in the hall near his Cambridge University office. His question to them was how they thought their experience would be different if the sun actually did go around the earth. The students, once over the initial shock of being accosted by a wild professor, realized that it probably would be no different from their current experience in which the earth went around the sun. For Wittgenstein the point was both that empirical evidence can be a mixed message and that interpretation is malleable and linked to systems in place through which the individual makes sense of the world. However, for our purposes, it points to the fact that trying to deduce abstract, though seemingly simple, principles of science (e.g., the earth goes around the sun) from empirical evidence gathered "willy-nilly" by the individual can be a challenging operation. Especially in a case, such as the Harvard oak tree, in which the empirical evidence, the "empty" air, points in exactly the opposite direction. It only takes a few moments to generate a fairly long list of fundamental scientific principles that seem incongruent with our experiences of the world. The notion that matter can neither be created nor destroyed seems challenging in light of boiling water or burning wood; laws of inertia and motion run up against lives lived in a gravity-filled vacuumless world; and the conservation of energy seems antithetical to our experience of cars running out of fuel and batteries dying on our Game Boys. Yet these abstract principles undergird much of what is taken for science and much of what is helpful in becoming a scientifically literate citizen. My argument is that in many classrooms, especially those of the earlier grade levels, we have blithely accepted the principle, derived from Rousseau and put through the grinder of Spencer, Dewey, and the ongoing varied incarnations of the progressive movement, that we must start with the child's experience and from that "empirical evidence" we help the child to deduce the abstract scientific principle. I am not arguing that teachers do not, or should not, provide wonderful classroom moments that help students to "experience" the principle in question, but I think that if this evidentiary issue is tied to the second problem, the "concrete versus abstract conundrum," the results of their few properly oriented experiences are simply outweighed by the children's empirical evidence. Water boiling away into empty air simply outweighs the evidence in the opposite direction. The result is that at this early level the myth outweighs the principle and solidifies in a child's understanding.

## The Concrete Versus Abstract Conundrum

What this second problem does is keep out of the hands of the children a central metaphor, a kind of lens, that allows them to make sense of and organize both their targeted classroom experiences in a science context and their other experiences in the rest-of-the-world context under the rubric of a meaningful scientific construct. Children are no longer stuck weighing two sets of seemingly contradictory evidence and selecting one or the other; they instead have a means of bringing all the evidence together into one framework. However, the reason this metaphor is kept out of the hands of children is that it is considered to be too abstract for them to handle. Education has drawn this idea out of the progressive movement and the work of psychologists such as Piaget. The idea, in simple terms, is that educators need to stick with the concrete, that which surrounds the children in their neighborhoods and homes, and wait until they reach a developmental level of abstraction at which they can handle the abstract concepts of life, the world, and science. Thus, we stick with what the students know and experience. However, beyond the fact that this seems to profoundly undervalue the sophistication of our children, this argument does not seem to be borne out in practical experience. Small children the world over and throughout history have been told stories about fantastical things, about humans transforming into animals, about animals talking, about different worlds, and we don't question their ability to make sense of these things that do not fall into the category of their realms of experience. But, more profound, many of these stories are fundamental mechanisms used by cultures to help shape the child's understanding of the world, fundamental and highly abstract mechanisms. These stories are filled with love, hate, justice, value, evil, and goodness, and we accept that children are making sense of these ideas as we see them both recapitulated and, more important, manipulated in their play and in other interactions with the outside world. On a side note, often these stories have poor science in them as well. So why is it that we are fine with providing these highly abstract guiding metaphors for life to young children and yet we balk when it comes to providing less significant, maybe, though equally useful, metaphors for science, or other subject areas, for that matter, in school? In 3-year-olds, no one expects full functional use, or the provision of its entire complexity, of the concept of justice, although some are exceedingly adept with it—but no one seems to advocate that children not encounter the concept. One wonders whether that would be possible. The same seems to apply to these scientific concepts. The question is not yes or no to the abstract but the means through which the abstract is made available.

Thus, it is these two problematic beliefs, child-centered empirical evidence and concrete versus abstract, in conjunction that continue to play the underlying role in limiting scientific literacy. It is important to remember that I am not trying to stop giving children experiences or having them make sense of their own experiences. What I have been arguing, and what will form the underlying argument for the imaginative classrooms I will discuss next, is that we also need to provide the means, the tools, and the concepts to make sense of those experiences. The other caveat I want to offer and that I hope will become apparent is that I am not simply advocating that we drop a university science curriculum onto the heads of 8-year-old children and be done with it. As with the example of abstract notions of justice given to young children, the answer seems to lie in making the abstraction available, knowing—and this is the power and wonder of the abstract—that it will reappear and need to be reexamined, reworked, and regenerated on an ongoing basis for much of the rest of our lives. It would make sense, it seems, that there might be difficulty in assuming that a child will be able to deduce, from his or her own obviously limited experiences, abstract ideas that took multiple generations of fairly bright members of humanity thinking hard on the subject to generate in the first place.

# A POSSIBLE SOLUTION:
## THE IMAGINATIVE SCIENCE EDUCATION

*Scene I*

Picture this: The classroom is abuzz. There are 25 children in a circle, engaged in what looks like a ritual dance. In the center of the circle stands a child dressed in yellow, arms outstretched to resemble the rays of the sun reaching out into the universe. Around the sun 24 earths revolve following a trajectory that replicates the appropriate orbit. Along with this, students assist one another in getting their axial tilts in the correct directions as the earth spins and leans through space. For the children this is the dramatic center of a curriculum unit that begins with the story of a sometimes alienated child, maintaining her orbit about the family and yet leaning in and out depending on their acceptance of the situation and the number of chores required. The unit continues with the creation of clay models of the multiple characters in this galactic community and ends with copious drawing and writing as the students articulate their learnings, understandings, and ongoing questions. The students, through the depth of their imaginative engagement with the earth's story, are caught up in their wonder, and teaching itself has become fun and regenerative for their teacher.

*Scene II*

This classroom is quieter. Small groups of students are working together in various corners trying to make sense of the extraordinary lives of Galileo, Linnaeus, and Marie Curie. What was the world of science like into which they brought their radical ideas? How were those ideas received? And now that they have been accepted, what are the ramifications of those ideas? Beyond this, the students are following through on some of the experiments, tracing the many stories of a developing science, doing research on these heroic individuals, and preparing challenges for classmates to engage in that are a means to make sense of that science.

*Scene III*

This final classroom is in the local council chambers; council is in session. These 12th-grade students are putting the finishing touches on their presentation to the council about the level of pollutants in the local river that flows silently through the town's center, the likely sources of toxins, and some possible solutions. Two months of work, using sophisticated scientific equipment and a current experimental design, that began in response to a real local concern is culminating in this real-world experience. Here students are "doing" science at the very highest levels, but also encountering how science meets their community, the responsibility they must bear for their results, and the actions taken in accordance with those results. They are going to need to explain and defend their results and demonstrate that their science is good in the face of some serious opposition and that they have a grasp on the historical/political/sociological environment out of which this discussion has appeared. But the students must also be able to offer a critical understanding of the multiple perspectives involved, point to areas where they themselves are less than clear, and do all this under the sometimes harsh and emotional spotlight of politics. They are discovering and experiencing the edges of science, theory, perspective, and their community.

These three examples are drawn from very different classrooms but are taught by educators who think of themselves as being imaginative in the way we are trying to explore it here in this volume. Although none of these scenes, in and of themselves, seems to be that different from what many very good science teachers are doing today, the difference lies in the systematic K–12 consideration of how we come to most successfully learn. The result is that teachers are operating from the tools the students are bringing with them and that each teacher can see how what they are doing fits into a long-term project of becoming scientifically literate. The imagination has tended, in the quotidian world, to be associated with the arts, creativity, and flights of fancy. However, for our purposes we will think of it as the ability to think of the possible. The imagination is that which operates to make sense of the world in the area between raw empirical data, uninterpreted sensory inputs, and the Truth. The result of this huge space in which to operate is that the imagination is a very busy bee, especially given the way the Truth seems to be continually receding.

These three teachers are conscious and thoughtful about the developing imaginative capacities of the students (and themselves) and about recognizing the kinds of "imaginative tools" those students are bringing with them in order to make sense of their worlds. Their worlds are places they are immersed in, exchanging with, and continually trying to adjust to and make sense of. This ongoing active interchange between sentient and sensible is what philosopher Maurice Merleau-Ponty calls the "life-world" and is the very foundation out of which science arises. Ecophilosopher David Abram claims that science is a form of consensus building; it is one means that humanity has developed to try to make more uniform sense of the world. However, as he points out, modern Western science is only one way of making sense, a way that focuses on a particular, strangely detached idea of facts, theory, and truth. For Abrams, the result is that other ways of making sense of the world are marginalized. What these teachers are trying to do is to build a more robust sense of science that allows them to draw more completely on varying ways of making sense of the world. Our argument is that through the use of the imagination these multiple ways of making sense help to incorporate information and experiences more completely and ultimately give a more robust understanding to science itself. The imagination is the way to bridge the divide between empirical and technical information, seen so clearly in the Harvard example. The hope is that through the imaginative education of science, students become more inquisitive about their own process of discovery; more critical citizens; and, for those who chose, better scientists, for, as Einstein has recognized, "the greatest scientists are artists as well. Imagination is more important than knowledge. For knowledge is limited whereas imagination embraces the entire world" (Viereck, 1929). Thus, I plan to devote the rest of this chapter to offering, cursorily, a kind of framework for an imaginative science education. I will do this by using these three classroom examples to help us examine four ways of making sense of the world: mythic, somatic, romantic, and philosophic.

## Mythic Understanding of Science

Scene I is a grade-1-and-2 split, again not necessarily that different from many classrooms around the world except that the teacher, Ms. Martin, is considering the components of the lesson through an imaginative lens while keeping an eye on the two problems considered earlier. These young students are, for the sake of this discussion, predominantly oral in their orientation. Most of them possess fairly sophisticated oral tools that have been drawn from their environment, and they use, and are used by, those tools in order to understand the world. In other words, they have been oral for a while, they view their environment and themselves through the lens of orality, and they have some ability to manipulate the tools they do possess. Thus, Ms. Martin dials directly onto those aptitudes by using oral tools such as story, metaphor, rhyme, rhythm, and pattern to help students in her classroom. Because these are the preponderant tools of this age group, they are the ones used in order to gain better access to the curriculum. But this is not simply a gimmick. For example, the story is not just an emotional "hook" with which to gather attention, but the conscious use of a means the students possess in order to make important abstract scientific and curricular elements sensible, available, and retainable for those students. In this case, abstract concepts such as tilt, lean, rotation, and orbit are selected and focused upon so that once they are understood and experienced students will have a framework that allows them to organize other incoming empirical and nonempirical information. As a result, seasons, diurnal time, and the ongoing curriculum can be incorporated into a more complete framework rather than leaving the student in the dissonant position of having to select between seemingly competing information.

A second example is the use of metaphor. The dramatic reenactment of sun and earth is a metaphor played out in a shrunken three-dimensional space. This ability to shift across metaphor and demonstrate understanding across multiple modes (e.g., in clay, in drama, in peer discussions) is one that not only is critical for more sophisticated thinking and experimentation but is also the very heart of the move from oral language to written, for what is T-R-E-E if not a metaphor of the sound we make, which is itself a metaphor for that actual object we encounter outside? Beyond this there are several other things to note. The first is repetition. Ms. Martin repeats the specific story multiple times, allowing students to hear and rehear in the process of their own image forming. This repetition combined with the transference, moving between mediums of reexpression, mentioned earlier, allows students to both gather and make their own knowledge from what is being offered. Second, Ms. Martin uses a narrative form across the unit by starting from a point of dissonance (e.g., the child figuring out how to fit within the family or wondering about the sun and earth) and ends with a kind of resolution (e.g., the child in orbit around his or her galactic family or an understanding of how the earth fits into orbit around the sun). Thus, she not only draws an affective connection to the learning the students are making, which is fundamental for engagement and retention, but she also models the process of scientific learning. A problem of importance to the child/scientist is posited and then through exploration and shifting perspectives/metaphors possible solutions and new understandings appear. The hope then is that students are no longer having experiences and science running at odds with each other but that the two are actually fitting into a larger conceptual framework that can "explain" both. I might argue, along with Abram (1996), that this is the point of scientific inquiry.

### Somatic Understanding of Science

Anyone who has spent time with small infants knows that they are deeply physical in their way of making sense of the world. Everything goes into their mouths, light fascinates them, and all their sounds are deeply embodied. What we seem to forget is how much the rest of us use our bodies—and our perceptions if you agree with Merleau-Ponty—to make sense of the world as well. We tie bits of string around our fingers to trigger memory, we feel depressed when it rains, and we understand others through their "body language" as much as through their words. It is also this empirical evidence gathered and made sense of through the body that is probably the largest contributor to the Harvard "folk knowledge" problem. We can see through all these examples ways in which the body is included in the project of learning. However, although we see the seniors practicing for their big council chambers event by trying to take on the personas of their dissenters to better prepare themselves, the translation is much more direct and expansive for the earlier grades, in which children are more formatively somatic in their way of understanding. Thus, the children all become embodied earths circling the sun, their hands are engaged in the creation of models, and in scene 2 they are physically engaged in doing some of the foundational experiments of scientific history.

These teachers are conscious that young children comprehend the world through their senses, through movement, through form, and through interaction and that it is important to robust scientific learning to engage them physically. There is also a recognition that within the context of teaching science, children often have a "body" of physical experience that may run counter to the concepts being taught. As such, classroom somatic learning must operate in support of the proposed concept and offer ways in which the other experiences can be understood so that they too can be incorporated. Children can, for example, physically become the acorn setting off on the journey of growing into an oak tree, but part of the action is to keep on "breathing" to bring in all the carbon dioxide they will need. Imagine a classroom where the kids are actually allowed to "inhale" their food. On a side note, this project becomes a nice way to see how tree and human grow together, exchanging the air necessary to continue to grow. This in turn becomes a nice entrée into key scientific and curricular elements dealing with ecology and the complex and cyclical nature of the world.

But by the time students have reached middle elementary school, they are almost completely immersed in the way of understanding that is dominant in Western culture and in our school systems. They are understanding the world through written language. For imaginative education this is not a bad thing so much as it is a change, which needs to be prepared for and recognized, in the way students are making sense of the world and the tools available to them to do that. Literacy is a way of understanding, a way in which most of us are immersed, that opens particular vistas and makes sense of the world in valuable ways. It also brings with it a whole new set of imaginative tools. However, although those tools build upon the previous ones, any new way of understanding does reconstitute the sense-making means available to us. This change of a way of understanding, then, in the words of Chet Bowers, prioritizes some kinds of knowing while also marginalizing other kinds. The same can be said for either the oral or the physical, but possibly the conspicuous dearth of the sophisticated physical and oral ways of understanding in today's Western world might be an indication of a need for more balance. It is a balance that imaginative science education is aiming for and that Einstein might have been pointing at in the quote given earlier.

## Romantic Understanding of Science

Gadamer and Wittgenstein both claim that the world is playing or shaping us at the same time we are shaping or playing it. This claim seems to be correct when we begin to talk about literacy. In fact, it may be helpful to think of literacy as a well-worn groove filled with time-honored tools that the culture has laid down for us to make sense of our surroundings. Unfortunately, sometimes we become so immersed in the groove that we ignore the fact that there are other ways of "playing" the world. Children developing literacy are intrigued by all things human; they are fascinated by the extremes and limits of the world; they are looking for reasons and rudimentary systems through collecting and organizing and as a result are less interested in magic (how does Santa Claus get down all those chimneys in one night?). This process of humanizing and framing the world also results in a deeper recognition of self, situated in space and time, as a becoming-independent entity. Thus, as we see in scene 2, students are getting a sense of science as a human endeavor. The teacher is engaging the tools geared toward the humanizing, the heroic, and the organizing by allowing students to gather, share, and collectively understand examples of the strivings of scientists. Underneath, students are learning more about the possibilities available to humanity as they begin to exercise their own developing independence.

Everything that we know in science was "discovered" by a human being and often the stories themselves are fascinating. Individual human beings overcome great challenges and dangers to discover something that can change the very fabric of the community. In conjunction we see students getting a sense of the cumulative process that is science. However, there is a very real danger here and that is the passive consumption of science. As with any huge change, such as the advent of literacy, there are obvious benefits, the ability to record and then revisit information. However, there are also always, although often unintended, downsides. Passive consumption without depth of understanding (e.g., "you just need to tell us what we need to know") is one of these and it is a real danger in the world of science education. There is the potential for knowledge to become something situated out there with an already extant correct answer and I just need to mumble the correct formulation and that will be construed as understanding. The best example I can think of is the demonstration-versus-experiment problem. How many times have we encountered situations in which something is called an experiment and sometimes the students' ideas about what is going to happen are sought out, but in actual fact, everybody knows that there is a right answer and that the demonstrator is going to carry out the demonstration before our eyes? The result is achieved and the dissenting opinions are lost. There is no scientific process going on; scientific knowledge already exists and we just need to listen for the answer. But science doesn't work that way and for 10-year-olds discovering and playing with buoyancy it is still an insight when they discover it for themselves, whether the rest of world knows it or not. Thus, science can be alive or dead; it can be a process of trying to make sense of the world or being told how it works; it can result in a deep understanding of the concepts or a superficial knowledge of fact.

## Philosophic Understanding of Science

In scene 3 high school seniors are trying to make sense of the world in a much more systematic way. For these students the tools of a philosophic way of understanding include generalization, theory formation, logical reasoning, and explanations of anomalies. Anyone who has worked with the all-knowing later adolescent has had experience with both their urge to find neat ways to tie everything together and their unmitigated ability to poke holes in any attempt to suggest something to the contrary. Albert Camus felt that one of the characteristics of humanity was to always want to instill order into the seeming chaos of the world we experience. For generations we have sought the neat packages, the larger systems, the metanarratives, the universal truths, and the creators who would help us to make sense of the world in a generalizable way. In many ways we are uncomfortable with ambiguity and want to be able to predict the future. This push to overarching truths is, quantum physics notwithstanding, the historical trajectory and currency of science today. It is also an important way of understanding the world. For students, such as those in scene 3, to be able to gather evidence, to join ideas together and link discoveries, and to ultimately discern a pattern that can explain and possibly predict what is to come in their world is an important skill. They must also be able to modify, change, and develop those theories as new information or conflicting opinions appear. This way of making sense of the world in metapatterns is key to understanding a part of the scientific project and to becoming a skilled consumer of science. This brings us to a second important component of this kind of science work: its worldliness. The kind of work being done by these students has real implications for real people, and that allows them to see that they are a part of a system of knowledge and decision making and that underneath the seeming detachedness of this science are real and complex lives being lived. Because, as Camus points out, we are never, no matter how we try, able to organize our world in a complete overarching and ordered way. Thus, between complete order and absolute chaos lies the zone of the human, the area that he calls the absurd and I am calling the imagination.

## CONCLUSION

I began this chapter by pointing out two problems in the current practice of science education and then proceeded to offer a possible solution that focuses upon the imagination. The imagination is a means by which the possessor creates a sense of the world. Imaginative teachers build upon the tools of the imagination that students have available to them in their particular and current way of understanding, whether it be mythic, somatic, romantic, or philosophic, to best allow them entrée into the concepts, knowledge, and ways of doing that is science in the best and most robust sense. No one makes sense of the world in one particular way from cradle to grave and it behooves us, as teachers, to take advantage of the ways of understanding and the tools that the students have available to them. We must also remember that these tools grow and develop and that moving from one way of making sense of the world to another is a process of both gain and loss. Last, for these three teachers there is a sense of how the work they do with their particular age group builds on what has come before and toward what is still to come. And so, although it has probably always been latent, except in the mind of Einstein, science and the imagination are officially joined.

*Chapter 7*

# Imagination
# and Arts Education in
# Cultural Contexts

## SHARON BAILIN

Imagination tends to be highly valued in contemporary Western society, particularly in the arts. As a consequence, growing educational attention is being paid to its development. We want people to have imagination, in the sense of possessing a particular ability or capacity that can be deployed in a variety of contexts. Having imagination in this sense is usually seen as desirable in and of itself in terms of the vividness of one's inner life and the richness of one's understanding (Egan, 1992b, pp. 45–65). But we also want people to have imagination so that what they produce will be imaginative. We want them to produce ideas that are original and unconventional, works that are freely created and genuine products of the person's inner being, products that carry the stamp of the individual. Thus there is a connection made between imagination and individuality, originality, freedom, and self-expression. There is the expectation that individuals possessed of a high degree of imagination will produce imaginative work.

In this chapter I shall look at these ideas regarding how we think about imagination in contemporary Western society and why we see it as valuable. In the first part, I shall examine some contemporary conceptions of imagination and raise some issues concerning the notion of imagination as a capacity, faculty, or process within the person. In the second part, I shall critically examine the idea that producing imaginative works is a matter of using imagination in this inner-capacity sense as well as the assumptions regarding individuality, originality, freedom, and self-expression that are associated with this idea. The latter I shall address by looking at other cultural contexts in which these assumptions are not present: Balinese dance and early Renaissance art. I shall conclude by drawing more general implications from my examination. Although the argument will be developed using examples from the arts, I think that lessons can be drawn from the analysis that have broader application.

## WHAT IS IMAGINATION?

It is virtually impossible to provide one unambiguous and uncontested definition for imagination. The term *imagination* and its cognates have had many different meanings historically and are still used in a variety of ways. The examination of the history and present state of the concept provided by Egan (1992b, pp. 9–43) will be useful in laying out some of its aspects and associations. I would agree with Egan that, although the various aspects do not coalesce to form a coherent conception, each has left traces that layer into the ways in which the concept is currently used (p. 9).

One basic sense of imagination, and one with long historical roots, relates to the act of imagining. Imagination, in this sense, is closely connected to the forming of mental images. Several contemporary theorists have pointed out that not all instances of imagination involve images or visualization (White, 1990, p. 188), but Egan (1992) argues that image-forming is common in conceptions of the imagination and "may in subtle ways be inevitably involved in all forms of imagining" (p. 43). Even if one does not agree with Egan on this last point, it does seem to be the case that vestigial traces of the image-forming notion do creep into other uses of the term.

Notions of unusualness and invention, of the fantastic and bizarre, also enter into some uses of imagination. Myth and fantasy are often deemed particularly imaginative because of the unusualness and vividness of the images portrayed. This sense of imagination, in focusing on the nature and quality of the images held, puts emphasis on the vividness and emotional quality of one's inner life, a theme that emerges frequently, particularly in educational discussions of imagination (Egan, 1992b).

One context in which the concept of imagination is sometimes deployed is with respect to how something is grasped or understood. To have one's imagination engaged in learning implies that one understands not just rationally but also holistically, viscerally, with vivid images and emotional associations. This is a primary sense in which theorists such as Egan advocate educational practices that engage and stimulate the imagination.

One essential sense of imagination focuses on generativity. Imagination, in this sense, involves generating possibilities, thinking of things as other than they are. White (1990), for example, defines imagination thus: "To imagine something is to *think of* it as possibly being so" (p. 185). Egan (1992b) characterizes it in terms of a flexibility of mind (p. 36). The generativity characteristic of imagination might include imagining possible futures and so having some possibility of changing the course of events, imagining other people's situations and so having empathy and tolerance, or imagining new ideas and so having the possibility of creativity and originality. There also seems to be some notion of quantity of ideas or possibilities connected with this sense of imagination. White (1990), for example, says that an "imaginative person is one with the ability to think of lots of possibilities, usually with some richness of detail" (p. 186).

These various senses of imagination do not unite to form a coherent conceptualization. Indeed, they can exist independently and may even conflict. The images that one forms in imagining, for example, may be quite commonplace, not at all bizarre or fantastic. The forming of images may not involve new possibilities but rather simply the revisualization of what one has previously seen. And the generation of possibilities may not involve images at all but rather nonvisual conceptualizations.

There are, nonetheless, some commonalities among the various senses. In all the conceptions, imagination is viewed as something within the person, as some sort of capacity that is common to all people but that some individuals possess to a higher degree. It is, moreover, a capacity that can be engaged, stimulated, and developed in general. Some theorists even argue that it can be developed apart from particular contexts through decontextualized techniques (such as visualization or brainstorming).

Imagination, in all senses described above, is a mental construct focusing on the mode and contents of ideation. Whatever else it may involve, it entails centrally the conjuring up of what is not present, be it images or possibilities.

Connected with virtually all these senses of imagination is some notion of originality. It is imagination that enables us to go beyond conventional thinking, to generate ideas that are truly new and our own, to express our individuality. The imagination is the font of one's personal generativity, the source of one's authentic vision, the crucible of one's individuality. Products of the imagination defy conventional ways of thinking and are manifestations of authenticity, freedom, and creativity. "Imagination," says Egan (1992b), is "the source of novelty, originality, and generativity" (p. 36). There is a high value placed on these qualities in modern Western societies, and our valuing of imagination is connected with this valuing.

## CRITIQUES

Historically there have been numerous critiques of conceptions of imagination that view it as some entity or inner faculty, as something within the person. Many such conceptions entail that the faculty or capacity of imagination can be developed through its exercise, much as one would develop muscular strength through exercising one's muscles. The problems that have been demonstrated with these conceptions point to the fallacy in believing that the imagination can be developed through various techniques, visualization, for example, which are independent of particular contexts, and that one will, as a consequence of undergoing such techniques, be more imaginative in any and all contexts.

One prominent example is the work of Gilbert Ryle, who as far back as 1949 presented an important critique of the main assumptions behind faculty psychology, pointing out the conceptual confusions involved in viewing the mind as an inner organ akin to physical organs and the related confusions in viewing mental concepts as inner entities existing within the mind (Ryle, 1949). He argued, rather, that mental concepts are attributed to people insofar as they perform mental acts in certain ways. According to Ryle, then, imagination does not refer to some inner entity or process, but is attributed with respect to the manner in which a wide variety of publicly observable actions are performed. He states:

> There are hosts of widely divergent sorts of behaviour in the conduct of which we should ordinarily and correctly be described as imaginative. The mendacious witness in the witness box, the inventor thinking out a new machine, the constructor of a romance, the child playing bears, and Henry Irving are all exercising their imaginations. . . . Nor do we say that they are all exercising their imaginations because we think that, embedded in a variety of often widely different operations, there is one common nuclear operation which all alike are performing. . . . [I]nventing a new machine is one way of being imaginative and playing bears is another. There is no special Faculty of Imagination, occupying itself single-mindedly in fancied viewings and hearings. (pp. 256–257).

Imagination, then, is attributed to people insofar as they think or act in an imaginative manner. As Barrow (1988) writes:

> People generally display imagination to varying degrees in various contexts, and to refer to someone with a well-developed visual imagination or sharp historical imagination is to talk about the manner of their visualizing or historical understanding rather than about some organ in the brain. (p. 80)

Whether or not one agrees with the reconceptualization of mental concepts entailed in these critiques and the removal of imagination from within the person, what is important for present purposes is the distinction between descriptive and normative senses of imagination to which they draw our attention. Descriptive senses, such as the ones we have been examining, attempt to describe imagination in terms of some inner mental capacities or processes. But because they focus on process and on the characteristics of modes of ideation, they can make no value judgments about their content. Whether an image is powerful or weak, whether a possibility is exciting or silly makes no difference for descriptive accounts. Such ideas or possibilities are all equally products of the generative capacity that descriptive accounts of the imagination are trying to capture.

But there is also a normative sense of imagination, captured in the adjectival form *imaginative*. And not all products of imagination are equally imaginative. The images one forms may be rich and novel, but they may also be simply replications of images one has seen. The possibilities one generates may be visionary but they may also be commonplace and cliché. Fantasies may be boring or ill wrought, one's imaginings of other people's situations insensitive, or one's vision for the future unworkable. The madman may display imagination in generating a great deal of nonsense. Calling a work imaginative implies not just that it is the product of a generative capacity, but also that it meets certain evaluative criteria. These evaluative criteria cannot be characterized by the process or capacity that may have led to their generation. They are, rather, given by the context.

In the arts, for example, what constitutes imaginative work may relate to content or to form. With respect to content, the vision expressed through a particular artistic interpretation may touch us, move us, reveal insights to which we can relate, thus prompting us to call it imaginative. With respect to form, artworks may manipulate sensuous elements such as color, tone, or rhythm in ways that are particularly effective both in the aesthetic effect on the audience and in solving particularly artistic problems posed by the discipline itself. Imaginative work is also possible in other disciplinary areas, including science, history, or mathematics, and even everyday contexts involving inquiry and problem solving. There are numerous ways to solve most problems, but some ways seem to be more interesting, innovative, original, elegant, or fruitful than others (Bailin, 1994).

It is clear, then, that what constitutes imaginative work varies greatly from area to area and is very much dependent on context. What is involved in being an imaginative sculptor is very different from what is involved in being an imaginative historian, and there is no reason to believe that being imaginative in one area is related to being imaginative in others. Imagination is not a power that can be developed on its own and then applied in a variety of contexts. Rather, being imaginative in an area very much depends on one's knowledge and skill within that area.

## THE CONNECTION BETWEEN
## IMAGINATION AND IMAGINATIVENESS

Once the distinction between the descriptive and normative senses of imagination is recognized, the question arises as to the connection between the two. The views about imagination that we have been examining make the assumption that imaginative works are products of imagination in the sense that they are products of a certain process or mode of ideation. Yet this is an assumption that needs to be examined.

Numerous theorists have noted the problems with the assumption that imaginative products necessarily arise from a particular type of process or can be characterized by the contents of their mode of ideation. With respect to the production of images, for example, the principal problem is that the production of mental images does not seem to be a necessary condition for producing imaginative work. Imaginative work takes place in many fields, philosophy or mathematics, for example, in which visual imagery does not play a prominent role (White, 1990). Nor are imaginative works necessarily bizarre or fantastic. Naturalistic paintings or realistic novels are just as likely to be thought of as imaginative as are fantasy novels or surrealist works (Barrow, 1988). Imaginative works are, indeed, the product of a process of generation, as suggested by the generativity sense of imagination, but so are all our works, imaginative or otherwise. Thus the production process cannot serve as the basis for picking out imaginative works (Barrow, 1988). The issue of fluency or quantity of production seems problematic as well. The idea that there is a connection between generating a large number of possibilities and producing imaginative work does not hold up under scrutiny. Creators frequently do not generate numerous possibilities in creating their works but because of their expertise can go right to the best ones (Bailin, 1994; Weisberg, 1993). There are, thus, reasons for viewing the assumed connection between creating imaginative work and an alleged imaginative capacity with some suspicion.

## INDIVIDUALITY, ORIGINALITY, FREEDOM, AND SELF-EXPRESSION

The second problem I want to look at concerns the idea that what one is doing in producing an imaginative work is expressing something within the person, expressing one's inner being, and producing something new and unconventional. The problems with these assumptions become salient when one compares these ideas about imagination with those in some other cultural contexts.

The connection between imagination and individuality, originality, freedom, and self-expression is very strong in contemporary society, particularly in the arts. But this connection is not universal. It is based, rather, on certain notions of persons and creativity that are particularly modern and Western. Taylor (1989) has argued that the modern Western worldview can be distinguished from the ancient and traditional by a particular conception of self that is characterized by inwardness, freedom, individuality, and being embedded in nature. The common contemporary conception of imagination, as described above, is marked by these same attributes. It is inward in being a psychological conception dealing with what goes on in people's minds. The Romantic emphasis on listening to the voice of nature within us added an emphasis on self-expression and emotion to the conception, and because such expression was seen as creating something truly new as opposed to merely imitating, notions of originality, individuality, and freedom were folded into the conception of imagination as well (Abrams, 1953; Furst, 1969).

Such notions were (and are) not, however, part of traditional worldviews and even in the West were a product of a gradual development (Taylor, 1989). Dissanayake (1995) argues, for example, that the ideas of genius, creative imagination, self-expression, originality, communication, and emotion are distinctively modern notions (p. 39). Traditionally art was not seen as "a private compulsion, a personal desire to mold or make something out of one's experience," the way moderns see it. It was, rather, for most of human history, an activity centered on communal meanings (p. 61).

## Example 1: Balinese Culture

Many of these assumptions about individuality, originality, freedom, and self-expressison do not obtain in some more traditional cultural contexts today. In traditional cultures, art is not separate from the rest of life but forms an integral part of important cultural practices. Meanings are given by context and tradition and an individual achieves his or her purposes in life only by working out these meanings in his or her individual existence (Jhanji, 1988, p. 162). Similarly, the traditional artist achieves the purposes of his or her art by re-enacting already existing paradigms. The aim is not the creation of novelty and the artist does not try to create a unique personal style or express his or her own emotions in a work. Originality, individuality, and self-expression are not what is at issue. As Jhanji (1988) explains:

> Contrary to making any claims to novelty the traditional artists make the opposite claim that nothing really novel is rendered by them; rather they are merely vehicles of projecting the primordial art forms. By definition all traditional art bases itself on certain conventions which are held important for its practice. Unlike his modern counterpart, a traditional artist is essentially working out through his art creation a primaeval form, laying out in advance the various stages for its creation. (p. 172)

A prime example of traditional art practice exists even today in Balinese culture. In Balinese society there is no separation between art and the rest of life or between artists and the rest of society. Rather, everyone engages in some form of art making and the passing on of the tradition is central.

Art is integral to daily life, religious celebration, and ritual practices. The types of objects and practices deemed as art in Western society and set apart from everyday life are completely integrated into Balinese life. Nor are artists seen as imaginative geniuses set apart from society. Rather, everyone engages in some form of art making, from mask carving and weaving; to taking part in the ritual dances of the temple ceremonies; to fashioning palm leaf decorations, daily offerings, or elaborate temple offerings. Craft traditions are passed on from generation to generation and entire villages are often devoted to a particular craft. Artistic practices are, thus, not viewed as the self-expression of an individual who defies tradition to create an original work. Rather, they are inseparably tied to religious beliefs and practices. Ritual dances, re-enacting ancient Balinese tales or the Hindu epic *Ramayana*, form part of the temple ceremonies, and elaborate masks are carved for these dances; stone sculpture adorns temples; and elaborately fashioned offerings are offered to the gods.

The religious/philosophical worldview that grounds these practices does not recognize a sharp qualitative difference between spiritual and material, supernatural and natural, or God and humanity. The religion of the Balinese is a particular version of Hinduism that is based on Indian Hinduism but has adapted the animistic tradition of indigenous people. Gods and goddesses are thought to be present in all things: the spirit world is regarded as a living force that must be reckoned with. Carefully crafted objects, for example masks or small doll-like figures, are thought to provide hosts for the cosmic life forces to take up residence when they come to earth to listen to human requests. Thus a ceremonial mask not only aids in visualizing divine powers but also provides them temporary material manifestations. Mask wearers, while engaging in ritual dances, are often believed to be possessed by these spirits. Masks are not art objects in the Western sense. Sacred masks are never displayed on walls but are kept in fabric bags, and mask carving is considered a sacred process (Belio, 1970; Covarrubias, 1932; Ramseyer, 1938; Slattum, 1992).

We can see, then, that in Balinese culture, novelty is not an aim, and individual self-expression is actively discouraged. A recent comparative study of American and Balinese artists noted this difference in values regarding artistic creation. While the Americans emphasized the self, self-perception, and self-expression, in their interviews, the Balinese saw their art as "a collective effort involving others, requiring devotion and offerings to the gods, and necessitating consideration of themes from sacred texts" (Gaines & Price-Williams, 1990, p. 109). The authors noted also "a tendency toward the generic and types in the work of the Balinese, with the personal psychology of the artist being relegated to the background" (p. 109). Differences were also noted in the nature and role of originality.

In contrast to the American obsession with authorship and authenticity, "copying the design of others is approved and is considered a compliment" for the Balinese (p. 108).

Notions of individuality, originality, free self-expression, or radical novelty are thus conspicuously absent from Balinese art making. This does not mean, however, that Balinese artists cannot be imaginative. Rather, their imaginativeness is exhibited in the manner in which they instantiate the pre-existing paradigms. As Jhanji (1988) states:

> For these artists, creativity lies in their transfiguring the eternal into images, in being original in the sense of turning to the original, the primaeval. (p. 169)

Weiner (2000) points out that this type of interpretation, although not focusing on novelty per se, may still be imaginative:

> The opposite of creativity is not tradition, but thoughtless habit and routine. Within a traditional framework, repetition of a pattern may or may not be a routine, mechanical process, it could also be an opportunity for personal interpretation of that pattern. (p. 153)

And further:

> The question is not whether the same pattern is constantly repeated, but whether or not the work is infused with a creative passion which results in a unique presentation of the traditional themes. . . . Having conventions of creativity and models to follow does not mean that an individual creator cannot be unique or that there are no differences in quality of the works. (pp. 154–155)

In a similar vein, Jhanji (1988) states:

> Needless to say that this priority to primordial forms did sometimes result in a mechanical duplication of artifacts based on ready-made recipes by mediocre artists. But this fact is often exaggerated by the enthusiasts of novelty in art. Traditional art forms do not set so much store by novelty and extraordinary creative independence as by a skilful and innovative use of already existing parameters of artistic excellence. (p. 170)

Moreover, despite the focus on tradition rather than novelty, Balinese arts do incorporate innovation and have had a history of change and development. A Topeng dancer, for example, may introduce his own style, variations, and improvisations into his performance once he has mastered his teacher's version of the dance (Spies & DeZoete, 1983; Slattum, 1992). Different ceremonial masks, although an instantiation of a particular traditional character and conforming to its general features, will not be exactly alike. And Balinese oral tradition attributes the present form of certain well-known masks to particular inspired individual carvers (Slattum, 1992).

## Example 2: Renaissance Art

Although the assumptions regarding the centrality of individuality, originality, freedom, and self-expression for imagination are prominent in Western cultures today, prior to the Renaissance these assumptions did not play a significant role. Art was not seen as the manifestation of something within the artist. Rather, artistic activity had to do with the making of purely functional artifacts. Painters and sculptors were viewed as craftspeople whose skill was acquired by apprenticeship to a master and immersion in the tradition. Individuality was not a significant consideration. All artisans were members of guilds and the creation of art was usually a collective process and more often than not anonymous. Nor were artworks seen as the manifestation of individual self-expression. Rather, art was made in response to the demands of patrons, who also determined the specific content and imagery. Art making was not about individuality, originality, freedom, or self-expression.

During the course of the Renaissance, the arts underwent a dramatic transformation toward an astonishing naturalism, which allowed for unprecedented expressive possibilities. Concurrent with these changes in the content of the visual arts, there emerged an altered conception of artistic activity and a new role for the painter (sculptor or architect)—that of artist. Art making was elevated from its position as manual labor and granted new respect and prestige. Individual artists were recognized and sought after and gained more autonomy. Terms such as *invention, genius,* and *imagination* were applied to their work.

The popular explanation of why the nature and practice of the arts changed in this significant way during this time is that the era was blessed with a few geniuses, exceptional individuals of extraordinary talent, creativity, and insight who effected these changes through the power of their imagination.

I would argue, however, that the situation is much more complex than this description would imply. There were, in fact, many factors involved in these changes in the arts, factors that were interconnected in a complex web of relationships:

1. An economic boom that generated considerable wealth that could be spent on art, a well-educated and cultured elite to support its production, and a resultant concentration of artistic talent that promoted excellence and a unity of artistic criteria;

2. The emergence of humanism, which focused on antiquity, on a rediscovery of the thought and achievements of ancient Greece and Rome that was central to the development of Renaissance art and that provided models of classical works and techniques to be copied and imitated;

3. A humanist philosophy that stressed human dignity and freedom and opened up the possibility for scientific observation and the development of sciences such as mathematics, anatomy, optics, geometry, mechanics, and color and light theory, all of which had a profound influence on the arts;

4. The emergence of a new goal (or rather, the rediscovery of an ancient goal) for painting—mimesis, or imitation, and increasing achievements in naturalistic portrayal;

5. Numerous scientific and technical advances, including the invention of oil paint, which made possible the layering of paint, creating many of the expressive effects characteristic of Renaissance painting, and also including the discovery (or rediscovery) of linear perspective, which allowed the creation of spatial illusion and made naturalistic expression possible;

6. The training of artists, which was extremely rigorous and required copying masterworks, models, and ancient pieces as well as rendering live models (the emphasis was on the mastery of technique, not on originality);

7. A concerted effort by artists themselves to change how art was seen by working to gain recognition for the intellectual aspects of their work;

8. A transformation in the relationship between artist and patron, with patrons beginning to grant artists some leeway for creative invention;

9. The work of the artist and art critic Giorgio Vasari, whose writing was principally responsible for the construction of Leonardo and Michelangelo as creative geniuses, an ascription which was taken up in subsequent writing. (Ames-Lewis, 2000; Barzun, 2000; Boorstin, 1992; King, 2000; Kristeller, 1990; Turner, 1992)

The preceding examination demonstrates how the Renaissance changed the role of individuality, originality, freedom, and self-expression in art. Nonetheless, it appears that the view of imagination and its role in art was still some distance from our modern conception. One area in which this difference can be seen is with respect to the idea of originality. Originality was not primarily at issue in Renaissance art. So many innovations were, in fact, rediscoveries from antiquity, and this was seen not as a problematic lack of originality but rather as desirable. And the principal method of training and working was through copying and imitation, including copying from model books and from the works of other artists (Ames-Lewis, 2000; Turner, 1997).

The contemporary sense of artistic imagination as conjuring up something new from the artist's inner being is likewise absent from Renaissance art theory. The goal of art was not individual creativity but *mimesis,* or imitation. Artists were not trying to generate possibilities or to conjure up something new. Rather, their goal was to capture reality, both representing appearances and mirroring the hierarchical moral order of the world. And although there was a growing recognition of individuality of style, it was still generally distrusted. Alberti, for example, regarded it as "a limitation to be overcome by the universal artist rather than as a welcome expression of individuality" (Kemp, 1977, p. 390). Similarly, Leonardo states: "The idiosyncrasies of individual judgment must be overridden by absolute standards derived from a rigorous investigation of natural law" (quoted in Kemp, 1977, pp. 390–391).

Renaissance art was built on the ideas that mimesis of nature was of paramount importance, that art required rational knowledge, and that antiquity provided the best possible guide for achieving these ends. Invention and imagination were never to override these basic principles of art (p. 396).

Although the Renaissance did see an increase in the autonomy of artists over their work, it was never complete freedom in the sense of what is desirable in the contemporary art context. The idea of free will, which was being developed philosophically, was a limited one, and artistic and social constraints on the artist were still considerable. The extent of artistic license was still severely constrained, and most works were still done for commissions (Welch, 1997).

Although contemporary notions of artworks as unconstrained products of the artist's imagination or authentic expressions of the artist's inner being are not applicable to Renaissance art, we deem a very large number of the works produced during this period to be highly imaginative, some even exemplars of imaginative portrayal. This results, to a large extent, from the advances in naturalism, which allowed for unprecedented expressiveness in the works. Thus the imaginativeness of the works was connected with a series of contextual, intellectual, artistic, and social factors, many of which were external to the artist. The idea that art changed as a result of the extraordinary imagination of a few creative geniuses is highly problematic. Rather, the very idea of creative genius seems to have been largely a construction of writers such as Vasari and others who followed his lead to promote certain views about the arts. Rather than seeing imagination as a specifiable faculty that suddenly flourished during the Renaissance and that enabled certain individuals to effect radical changes, it might be more accurate to think of the concept of imagination and related concepts such as invention and genius as constructed and transformed in the process of these changes (Bailin, 2003).

This is not at all to deny that some (indeed many) of the artists of the Renaissance were extraordinarily talented, dedicated, and far-sighted individuals who wrought significant changes in their art and achieved work of unsurpassing beauty and expressive power. But a better way to think about what these individuals possessed might be in terms of a combination of abilities and traits, fueled by a rich and extensive repertoire of knowledge and developed through rigorous training, which interacted with contextual, intellectual, artistic, and social factors, to produce innovative and imaginative work.

Neither in the case of Balinese dance nor in the case of Renaissance art does art making seem to be about novelty, generating many possibilities, or individual self-expression. It focused, rather, on contributing to the tradition. Nonetheless I would argue that the work produced in these contexts can be viewed as imaginative, the latter having to do with the effectiveness of the manner of portrayal or performance. Imagination, viewed in this way, is inextricably bound up with the mastery of the artistic repertoire. And artists who produce imaginative work must be deemed imaginative.

## FOSTERING IMAGINATIVENESS

Before going on to lay out the implications of my analysis for fostering imagination, it will be helpful to review the arguments to this point. I began by describing our contemporary conception of imagination as seen as the capacity to generate possibilities, with strong associations of vivid imagery, powerful emotions, and a rich mental life folded into the concept. It is further assumed that this imaginative capacity possessed in high degree will lead to the production of imaginative works. We value imagination largely for its connection with individuality, originality, freedom, and authentic self-expression, qualities which are fundamental in modern societies.

I have pointed out some of the problems with the capacity sense of imagination, the most important for our purposes being that the possession of any particular mental capacity does not necessarily lead to the creation of imaginative works. Moreover, the connection made in modern Western culture between imagination and individuality, originality, freedom, and self-expression is not universal but is the product of a process of construction based on a variety of factors, social as well as intellectual. What this tells us about imagination, then, is that our modern assumptions about self and the nature of the imagination are not necessary in thinking about the production of imaginative work.

What does all this mean for attempts to foster imagination? First, it appears that focusing on the imagination as a generic faculty or set of mental processes will not necessarily lead to imaginative outcomes. Imagination is not something that can be developed in and of itself through decontextualized techniques such as visualization, generating large numbers of ideas, or focusing on novelty.

Rather, what is seen as constituting imaginative work will vary according to the context. As Barrow (1998) stated earlier, what is involved in being an imaginative sculptor is quite different from what is involved in being an imaginative historian. Thus what is central educationally is a deep understanding of the disciplinary repertoire and a high level of skill in its execution.

What constitutes imaginativeness will vary not only with disciplinary context, but also with cultural context. The equating of imaginativeness with novelty and individual self-expression reflects particularly modern and Western values. In traditional societies imaginativeness has more to do with how one instantiates and reinterprets traditional forms.

The assimilation of notions of individuality, originality, and free self-expression into the modern concept of imagination was the product of a gradual historical development and was affected by numerous economic, sociocultural, technological, and intellectual factors. Early stages of this development are evident in the Renaissance and further aspects have been added since, most notably in the Romantic era (Abrams, 1953; Furst, 1969).

Modern notions of imagination are still very much tied in with broader social and cultural conditions and values. Dissanayake (1995) notes the extent to which our modern Western notion of art "is dependent on and intertwined with ideas of commerce, commodity, ownership, history, progress, specialization, and individuality" (p. 40). The concern for originality, for example, is connected with notions of ownership and the commodification of art, aesthetic individualism has links to economic and political individualism, and the focus on self and freedom is a reflection of a social move away from community and communally determined meanings.

The recognition that our conception of imagination has a history and is tied to social and cultural circumstances does not, of course, invalidate its accuracy or usefulness. But this recognition does allow us some critical purchase on aspects of the conception. And upon examination it becomes clear that our modern conception of imagination tends to emphasize only one end of the continuum that characterizes imaginative work. It emphasizes radical novelty and discontinuity, but all innovations, however new, arise from a tradition and exhibit continuity with what came before (Bailin, 1994). It emphasizes freedom, but freedom is not and could not ever be total. One is always working within constraints of a disciplinary as well as social nature, and these provide the framework within which imaginative work is possible. For example, the artistic standards set by the guilds during the Renaissance have been replaced in modern times by standards set by academies, museums, and art critics (Dissanayake 1995, p. 196). Moreover, the demand for novelty has itself become a constraint in contemporary art. The modern conception of imagination emphasizes individuality, but this fails to acknowledge the role played by context and community in all imaginative work. It also emphasizes self-expression, but contemporary theorists have pointed out that the self is never isolated and free floating; rather it is constituted by its context, form of life, and interaction with ongoing cultural conversations (Taylor, 1989).

Once it is recognized that the modern conception of imagination is a cultural construction and not the description of a fixed psychological reality, the possibility is opened up of questioning the values and debating the practices promulgated in its name. And such questioning is becoming a feature of some contemporary arts practice. Some feminist artists, for example, are rejecting the exclusive focus on individuality by working collaboratively and even anonymously. Felshin (1995) points out that many activist art groups either

> prefer to remain anonymous [or] have opted for group names, thus challenging art-world notions of individual authorship, private expression, and the cult of the artist. . . . The fact that the composition of many of these groups shifts over time . . . further underscores the activist deemphasis of notions of independent expression and authorship. (p. 11)

And the uses of new electronic technologies for artistic reproduction have put into question our conventional notions of originality and authorship. McLuhan put the point thus: "As new technologies come into play, people are less and less convinced of the importance of self-expression. Teamwork succeeds private efforts" (McLuhan, quoted in Felshin, 1995, p.11).

The possibility for imaginative work exists in the dynamic tension between innovation and tradition, freedom and constraint, individuality and collaboration, the inward and the outward. If imagination is a continually evolving concept, then perhaps it has evolved too far in one direction. Now, I certainly endorse the importance of innovation, individual autonomy, and free expression. I am certainly not advocating suppressing the individual, mindlessly obeying tradition, or ignoring the inner life and quality of learning of the person. Rather, I am arguing that we need to heed the lessons from Balinese dance and Renaissance art. Imagination needs to exist in a dynamic tension between the poles described above. The picture of imaginative work as arising from an isolated individual self freely expressing and generating from the contents of his or her own psyche is inaccurate and misleading. It needs to be corrected by the recognition of the person as situated in a community, immersed in a form of life, and affected by social and cultural conditions, who assimilates the cognitive tools and cultural repertoire of the society and creates imaginative works out of an active conversation with the traditions of the culture in all their richness, detail, and diversity. These must play a central role in education for imagination.

*Chapter 8*

# "'Maginin' Some Peepin'": Imagination and Education for At-Risk Youth

## ANDREW SCHOFIELD

Jag's passion is freestyle rapping. As his teacher in a youth literacy program, I one day asked Jag how he maintained the rhyme and coherence of a rapped moment (which can last more 20 minutes). Jag commented, "Yo. Yo.[1] Ize go about 'maginin' some peepin'."[2] Jag's rap and his response reflect his world and the real and imagined resistance to drug addiction and family dislocation that shapes his life. Another student, when introducing an anthology of his own poetry, writes:

> My name is Scott Maloney. I live in B.C. Canada but hang out everywhere. I love the feeling of the street because only a few people know how it works—it has its own mind. [In my writing] I am trying to show everyone what it's like to be on the street and around it. (Moloney, 2002, p. 3)

While Jag's rap speaks to the intersection of imagination, biography, and pedagogy, Scott's anthology illustrates the integration of biography, his imaginative cultural representations, an adolescent's understandings of right and wrong, and his reading of life "on the street." He continues, "I came from it and it still interests me, of how it works because you could be out there for years and years and you still have no idea of how it worked" (interview, March 13, 2002). Both students draw on multiple genres that include spoken words, out-of-school literacies, conventional texts, and multimedia. Their classwork shows how imagination, social context, biography, teaching, and learning intersect in the lives of at-risk youth. I explore this intersection in the chapter.

### SCHOOL, CLASSROOM, AND COMMUNITY CONTEXT

In an interview digitally videoed and edited by a peer, Kuresh commented: "The classroom's not like a normal classroom. It's more like a home, a church almost. We're more of a community" (interview, April 18, 2003). While churches abound, homes and communities don't come easy in Kuresh's world: The school's local environment is predominantly low income and has a reputation for its high crime rate and litany of social problems (Surrey Social Futures, 2005).

The classroom and youth literacy program that Kuresh refers to, and on which this chapter is based, is located in a Learning Center. The Learning Center was established in August 2000 and is one of 125 public schools in a school district with 61,000 students—the largest in British Columbia and one of the fastest growing in Canada. In the school district, five Learning Centers have been established, each providing focused support to predominantly at-risk students[3] within the school district, offering students the chance to earn their Grade 10 and 12 graduation.

Students (who range in age from 15 to 21 years) at the Learning Center face a number of problems. For example, more than 7% of Learning Center students live independently (generally, on the street) at some point in the school year. On average four students each month are entering or being discharged from a local youth detention center and more than half the students experience violence as part of their daily lives, either at home or on the streets. More than 60% of the students indicated that a focal point for their social interaction was a Sky train station, a site plagued with problems related to youth crime, drugs, and violence (Canadian Centre for Education Alternatives, 1999, p. 2). In a random survey conducted by a literacy-class student, 64% of the learning center's morning-group students had not eaten breakfast and had not eaten any food by 11:00 a.m.

Principals in the school district annually identify students who, in addition to their at risk designation, have exceedingly low literacy and numeracy scores on provincial standardized assessment tests. At-risk students with low literacy levels throughout the school district are referred to the Learning Center's youth literacy program. For example, in provincial standardized assessment tests students in the literacy program score five grades below average in reading comprehension and six grades below average for numeracy; more than 25% of all assessments in reading comprehension score at or below the fifth-grade level, 30% of Learning Center students drop out because of literacy-based concerns, and 60% of the students in the literacy program have diagnosed learning disabilities, attention deficit disorders, or both.

The youth literacy program accommodates 32 students, mainly boys, who are divided into morning and afternoon sessions. The blend of students, with a range of literacy and numeracy levels and diverse life experiences, are enrolled and placed in the classroom on a full-time basis. Students are free to leave the program and the learning center, at which point new students are accepted. Continual entry and leaving, and the particularities of each student's life, require a flexible teaching process that includes individualized, group, and peer literacy support and instruction.

On arrival at school, students and I discuss their graduation options and intentions. Together we establish an academic plan, which can be modified during the course of the academic year. Students generally begin with a Grade 10 English course, but after about 3 weeks students generally switch to a grade 10 science or math program because of the greater structure that these courses offer. Finally students complete grade 10 social studies and career and personal planning courses.

The youth literacy program goes beyond the traditional literacies by teaching literacy through integrating the oral imagination, material contexts, and biographies of student lives; traditional "text-based" foci of reading and writing literacies; and opportunities for students to express themselves across multiple literacies. Student biographies are founded on the material contexts and events of their lives, and on the student's own readings and rereadings of these biographies. Below, I examine how the approach is applied.

## CLASSROOM APPLICATIONS

The case study presented here revolves around the work of two students, Aaron and Bryan. Aaron is completing his Grade 10, and Bryan his Grade 12. Bryan joined the literacy class in August 2000, and Aaron in March 2002. Bryan needed to read a novel as part of the course requirements of Communications 12; Aaron was struggling to connect to the First Nations studies components of Socials 10. Aaron is a strong reader with a clear grasp of symbolism and metaphor; Bryan is a committed and dedicated researcher, who, after working a night shift cleaning oven extractor vents in hotel kitchens, arrives at school willing to study. In October 2002 I encouraged Bryan and Aaron to work together on a collaborative piece of work that drew on their imagined and real biographies and on the representations of Maori culture captured in the novel *The Whale Rider* (Ihimaera, 1987).

The novel tells the story of Kahu, an eight-year-old Maori girl, and her great-grandfather, Koro Apirana. Koro, the elder chief of his community, struggles to reconcile his traditional beliefs regarding paternal hereditary leadership with the fact that his eldest son had left the community, leaving Kahu as potentially the next tribal leader. Koro starts a village school opened only to the boys to teach them Maori lore and etiquette. Kahu tries to join the school and is rejected and humiliated by her great-grandfather.

Eventually she earns his respect and he recognizes that "she was the one" (p. 145). I knew that both students would be able to identify with Kahu. This identification with the identity struggles of a girl would be an important learning experience for my students, who are socialized for the most part into the gendered mores of mainstream British Columbia and ignore (in different ways) the anomalies of gender experience and identity.

Knowing that Bryan was struggling to understand aspects of the novel's symbolism, I waited for him to read about half the novel before I brought in the film version. I encouraged Bryan to watch the film along with Aaron. At this point I was working with two of Egan's frameworks—for Bryan, the Philosophic and for Aaron, the Romantic. I anticipated that as the series of lessons progressed Aaron would engage in an increasingly Philosophic (and Somatic), and Bryan an increasingly Romantic, series of activities.

When the film was finished I asked the two boys to write me a film appreciation piece. Both students worked assiduously on this project: Occasionally they discussed parts of the film with each other; at other times we discussed the film together using dyad and triad organograms on the whiteboard.

Aaron read the novel with an interest that he had never previously shown, and Bryan wrote (all errors are in the original student writings):

> Wow that was a interesting movie. It was a lot to do with spirichal native stuff. I think the end was weard. They lift the boat on logs into the sea. . . . The grandfather was chef of their trib. Koro Apirana dident like the idea of Kahu being a leader because girls should not be a leader in the native culture. (Classwork exercise, January 12, 2003).

Aaron also emphasized spiritual aspects of Maori and Aboriginal cultures when he commented that

> I have always been interested in the native culture and history . . . they believe that their great loved one's spirits live within the whales but I am shure that it is also with othwe animals for example the eagle. I don't know much but the eagle is a big part of their religion. (Classwork exercise, January 12, 2003).

Aaron returned to this theme in his review of the novel. He observed that "by reading this book it has helped me relize how their religion works and how different things symbalize important things in their religion. Such as the whale sympolizes their gods and past chiefs" (classwork exercise, August 12, 2003).

Concluding his review of the film Aaron wrote:

It showed me that no matter what religion you are if you truly believe in your[self], you will be fine in life because if you fale at everything else in life like education or jobs and anything like that you can still have the pride and faith or spirit that you followed your religion and so when you die you can say you new who you really were and still die with dignity. (Classwork exercise, July 12, 2003)

A follow-up exercise emerged from a question that Bryan asked me: "Hey. What was those tattoos on that girl's face and on some of the men? And why were they sticking out their tongues in the one dance?" (Diary, March 12, 2003).

I responded by asking the students to prepare a short PowerPoint presentation using Internet and encyclopedia research on Maori dance and facial tattooing. The exercise lasted five hours, stretched over three days. The end product I received was a 90-second illustrated presentation on Maori dance, although in the students' written notes I saw that their research had included reading and note taking on the key features and symbolism of Maori facial tattoos. Reflecting on this aspect of their work, Bryan commented:

Aaron did most writing coz he's stronger at that than me. I did most research. I found all the pictures and got info on tattooing. Aaron wrote up the stuff and the big words. He's better with big words—like he came up with "concisely" on the one slide.
  I learnt lots of research skills on the Maori people. How they live and stuff. I lost stuff several times, so I learnt about patience, and good writing skills and backing up and saving when I typed it up and wrote it so many times. I revised "there" and "their" quite a bit of times to get them right. (Student reflection journal, September 12, 2003)

Although both students were responding to the Philosophic and existential arguments contained within the novel, I also wanted to see a deeper emotional understanding; I wanted the students to turn their reflection from a "distant" Aboriginal culture to, first, our own communities and, second, to our own lives. So, to deepen this emotional impact I turned to the Romantic Imagination through empathetic writing: The next exercise was to write two letters each. The first was to be from Kahu to her great-grandfather, Koro, expressing the impact on her emotions and self-esteem of his constant rejection. The second letter would detail his response.

At this point Bryan missed a week of school because of his work commitments, but I wanted to continue to link Aaron's interest in Maori culture with aspects of the First Nations experience in British Columbia. I gave him a short Stwomish story of how the Creator gave the gift of healing to humanity. Rather than asking Aaron to do a traditional reading and reading comprehension exercise—the type that had led to his early rejection of the institution of schooling—I presented him with a 6 × 10 inch piece of red cedar and a set of chisels, and asked Aaron to carve me a response.

Aaron asked how one could turn a story into a woodcarving or how a carving could be written as a story. He was unsure what to carve and what of the written version should be left out of his carving. He finally decided, after sketching several possible carvings, to develop his own symbolism and metaphor and not to worry too much if people didn't make a direct translation from his carving to the story.

With Aaron's carving I ended the unit of work. Throughout the different classroom exercises, Bryan, Aaron, and I discussed (often with other students who joined the conversation) that the central conflicts of the novel and film were tradition and change, patriarchy, youth identity, and elder values.[4] The projects were also drawn upon by other students in different ways. For example, Aaron's woodcarving was used by Youswe as the basis for short story writing, reading, and clay modeling. Youswe "read" Aaron's carving and made a clay model of what he understood from Aaron's design. Subsequently, building on a deepening emotional commitment to and renewed interest in school, Youswe then made a film version of the first two pages of Jose Saramago's (1997) novel *Blindness*. Aaron participated actively in the life of the class, acting in student films and serving as a camera operator and consultant. He started producing a film version of Isabel Allende's short story "Our Secret" (1991), before quitting school to get a job. Such was the case with Bryan: Two courses shy of his 12th-grade graduation, Bryan dropped out of school to work full time cleaning hotel and restaurant extractor vents.

In the next section I will explore the implications of the case study presented here in two domains of research: adolescent and youth literacy pedagogy, and Egan's (1997) Imaginative framework.

## YOUTH LITERACY: LITERACY, BIOGRAPHY, AND IMAGINATION

Literacy instruction at the secondary school level conventionally emphasises reading and writing instruction (Surrey School District, 2003), and much literacy analysis has focused on texts and processes of literacy acquisition. This "autonomous" model of literacy (Street, 1984) has been enriched by work on social and multiliteracy theories. Social literacies emphasize the "general cultural ways of utilizing written language" and see literacy as "situated" in the researcher's "interest . . . in social practices in which literacy has a role" (Barton & Hamilton, 2000, p. 7). Research examines the practices of literacy—the texts of daily, personal life. Throughout texts, reading and writing "are a crucial part of literacy events and the study of literacy is partly a study of texts and how they are produced and used. . . . *[L]iteracy is best understood as a set of social practices; these are observable in events which are mediated by written texts*" (Barton & Hamilton, 2000, p. 9; italics in the original).

Multiliteracy theory extends the definition of texts and literacy to include "multimodal" forms of representation and meaning making (Cope & Kalantzis, 2000, p. 5) and argues that not only should literacy pedagogy "now account for the burgeoning variety of text forms associated with information and multimedia technologies" (New London Group, 2000, p. 9) but also that schools need to design curricula to "mesh with different subjectivities, and with their attendant languages, discourses, and registers, and use these as a resource for learning" (p. 18). Social literacy (Barton, 1994; Street, 1995) and multiliteracy theories (Cope & Kalantzis, 2000) remind teachers that literacy practices are varied and situated across different media and that school-based literacy practices need to be inclusive of a broad range of students, cultures, and text formats.

With the insights of social and multiliteracy theories in mind I attempted to "rethink what we are teaching, and . . . what new learning needs literacy pedagogy might now address" (New London Group, 2000, p. 10). In this process I found social and multiliteracy theory silent when we turn to matters of imagination and biography (rather than identity) and actual pedagogic practices. To overcome this silence, and to get the students to read and write, I came to rely increasingly on oral and written imaginative play that emphasized mythic, heroic, and existential elements by rearticulating school texts into the narratives and biographies—stories—of the students' lives. I went beyond multiliteracy theory by observing, with O'Brien (1998), that for adolescents who struggle with literacy, and have been alienated from traditional secondary schools, issues of biography, resistance, and school literacy practices should foreground any approach to curricular innovation.

In this context it is important to recognize that biography and identity are different. Poststructural and multiliteracy theorists argue that "people are simultaneously members of multiple lifeworlds, so their *identities* have multiple layers that are in complex relation to each other"[5] (New London Group, 2000, p. 17; italics added). This notion of identity, as being discursively or materially constituted and (more important) being woven integrally into a person's consciousness, is one component of the notion of "biography." Biography refers, in addition to the different identities that one assumes, to the readings of those identities that one makes. For example, while aspects of my identity are apparent (my gender and ethnicity), my biography remains a story that I selectively tell. This telling is contingent on my memory and my imagination, audience, and context.

This approach to pedagogy integrates the grades 10–12 curriculum with the biographies and imaginations of at-risk designated adolescents. The approaches extend current notions of "adolescent literacy," "multiliteracy" theory, and the "imaginative framework" model (Egan, 1997) by moving away from the emphasis on reading, writing, and texts toward a braiding of text into narratives—stories written on the playing fields of curriculum by drawing on adolescent biographies and their multiple and hybrid identities and imaginations. Youth literacy pedagogy necessarily includes understanding youth as engaging in a play of biography, resistance, and imagination within the context of curricular content and the institutional norms of schooling (Alvermann, 2001; Cope & Kalantzis, 2000; McCarthey & Moje, 2002). Integrating these understandings of youth identity within a framework that is defined by orality, imagination, and text literacies, and that where possible draws on any available technologies to facilitate learning, defines youth literacy pedagogy, and brings the imaginative education framework to life.


## CONCLUSION

Youth literacy pedagogy encourages students to develop a sense of the power of written expression through the conventions of various literary and popular genres and content knowledge, while curriculum, biography, and imagination anchor instruction. This process is never complete and is constantly fragile. Moment by moment, at-risk students recreate and reinvent their own power. They display or withdraw literacy acts, discourses, or both, and for some, and only for some of the time, literacy can momentarily be a "transformative act [that] begins to assume an active and decisive participation" (Freire & Macedo, 1987, p. 54).


## NOTES

1. Accompanied by an enthusiastic, repeated hand pointing down gesture.
2. Hey. I just go about [it] by imagining some speaking.
3. District counselors, learning and behavior psychologists, and principals make the *at-risk* designations. Moderate (classified 323) and severe (classified 333) designations are made. Students with behavior "difficulties" are labeled 323; 333s are students with external agency support.

4. These conflicts climax at several points in the novel and film. One of these, occurring in the film but not the novel, leads Koro Apirana to ask Kahu: "What have you done?" only to be recanted at the end with Koro's comment to Kahu: "Wise leader forgive me, I am just a fledgling."

5. The genesis of these differences for the two groups is naturally quite different. For poststructuralists, difference is created by the textual nature of society and discourse; for multiliteracy theorists, difference is generated through an individual's affiliation to different communities—work, ethnicity, gender, recreational, and so on.

*Chapter 9*

# Imaginative Multicultural Education: Notes Toward an Inclusive Theory

## MARK FETTES

It is a common observation that schools have changed little over the past 100 years or so, in most of the ways that truly matter. Classrooms, pedagogy, curriculum, timetabling, and rewards and punishment—all of these have undergone periodic revision, yet the basic attitudes and beliefs underlying them have proved remarkably resistant to change. For instance, both John Goodlad (1989) in the United States and Cedric Cullingford (1991) in the United Kingdom have found that students are consistently cast in passive roles for most of their time in school, spending much of their time listening to teachers or waiting for something to happen. In this respect, as in many others, today's classrooms would be perfectly familiar to teachers and students of the early 1900s.

Yet there is at least one change, in the urban schools that now account for the large majority of students across the industrialized world, that would surely be noticeable and even shocking to such observers. Ethnic, linguistic, and religious diversity is now part of the fabric of school life. The intervening century has been one of massive economic migration and global population displacement caused by war, famine, or natural disasters; new communication technologies; rapidly expanding international travel; and steady urbanization. These and other forces have given rise to an extraordinarily varied population, both resident and transient, in the world's economic and cultural centers. And in their classrooms.

How significant is this fact? To judge from much of the educational literature, not very. The functional vocabulary of schooling is built on categories that take little account of social and cultural diversity. At best, diversity is constructed individually, in terms of "intelligence," "learning (dis)ability," "personality," and "behavior." In this context, one must recall that one of the core purposes of public education, from its earliest days, was to *transcend* difference: to provide children of every class and ethnic group with common cultural and technological resources that would tie them into the symbolic and material economies of the nation. As the products and inheritors of such traditions, educators tend to see diversity merely as a set of problems to be overcome, an array of hurdles on a racetrack that still leads to the same finish line.

There is, perhaps, little that can be said to change this conviction among those determined to hang on to it. Education is always as much concerned with what *ought to be* as with what *is*; the mere existence of diverse classrooms does not require us to treat diversity as an educational good. I want to argue, however, that we would be wise to regard it as an educational *opportunity*. Not only an opportunity to teach and learn different things, but also a chance to reconsider our taken-for-granted conceptions of teaching and learning. Diversity can throw a strong light into overlooked nooks and crannies of the classroom, dim corners we have preferred to ignore—including the uncomfortable clutter beneath our own desks.

Our reluctance to undertake such an examination, as reflected in the relatively marginal status of "multicultural" themes in the educational literature, is rooted in what Mikhail Bakhtin (1981) refers to as the "centripetal" forces of modern culture. Enormous efforts have been made over the past four centuries to develop predictability and reliability in human affairs; very often, this has involved one group of people imposing its ways of thinking and speaking, its beliefs, customs, and laws, upon many others. As Bakhtin and other critics have noted, this focus on centralization and unification, woven as it is into the very fabric of our lives (economic, political, linguistic, and others), has exacted an epistemological price. On a vast array of subjects, from our psychological makeup to the life and death of galaxies, we depend on the words and thoughts of influential but distant others as a guide to what is real and true. It is a condition simultaneously enriching and alienating, for it brings us into contact with an extraordinary wealth of knowledge, while constantly depreciating the particulars of our own experience (Smith, 1990). Yet diversity consists precisely of such particulars. Many have felt that to privilege diversity is to turn education on its head, to abandon the hard-won gains of the Enlightenment and undermine the ideals that hold modern culture together.

The persuasive force of this idea depends, in part, on whether one feels that education as currently practiced is in fact enriching our lives and our culture. If it is not—if findings such as those of Goodlad and Cullingford, cited above, are in fact a fairly accurate portrayal of most school experience for most children—then it may be that the idea is sound enough, and it is only its implementation that we have to work on; or it may be wrong in some more fundamental way. The first position seems to be that of most educational researchers. I will argue for the second. My approach is to show that diversity simply amplifies certain kinds of difficulty that inhere in modern education, to develop a conception of multicultural education that addresses these difficulties, and to illustrate the kind of conceptual and empirical research that such an approach requires. As one would expect, given the theme of this collection, imagination will play a critical role in the argument; but first the stage must be set for its entrance.

## THE DYNAMICS OF MODERNITY

One approach to thinking holistically and inclusively about education takes as its focus the so-called pedagogical triangle—the relationship of teacher, learner, and subject matter (or "I, Thou, and It" from Hawkins, 1974). One of the effects of modernity and its rage for order is to narrow down our vision of each of these and of the relationship between them.

To focus first of all on the two human elements of the triangle, the "I" of the teacher and the "Thou" of the student may be understood purely in individual terms, or in terms of their roles, rather than in a broader cultural and institutional context. The relationship between them can correspondingly be viewed, and experienced, as an encounter between two individuals or as a simple role relationship, neither of which need challenge or change the identity of each. Clearly there are significant incentives for teachers and students to buy into such an understanding, unless it is seen as directly contradicting the purpose of their encounter.

The "it," meanwhile, ties learning to the processes of knowledge and culture production in the broader society, which typically take place elsewhere than in the school. This means that subject matter in the classroom is usually in the form of artifacts (texts or other objects) in which the creative process and its social context are not manifest. What is more, these artifacts are licensed to appear in schools by virtue of a curriculum, which is itself not under school control. The artifacts thus come vested with an authority of their own: the authority of sanctioned knowledge or cultural expertise. The teacher, in forming his or her relationship with this material, is thus presented with an easy source of authority and a strong disincentive to challenge it, as this risks undermining his or her own status in the classroom. The alliance of teacher and curriculum provides a model for learners that itself discourages inquiry beyond narrowly prescribed limits. And so the educational dynamic most characteristic of modernity is born: classrooms centered on teachers and texts, with little space for learners to bring anything of themselves or their backgrounds into the mix.

Progressive education, of course, has long sought to change this dynamic, as have various radical variants of progressivism. Typically this involves shifting the locus of knowledge production, at least partially, to the classroom, in the hope of developing a richer Thou-It relationship. As Basil Bernstein (1971) pointed out more than 30 years ago, however, to do this effectively entails a radical shift in organization: the removal (or at least diluting) of textual authority demands that some equivalent pedagogical drive be found (Bernstein concluded that a strong shared school culture was the only alternative to the "invisible pedagogy" of the teacher-centered class). The risk of progressivism is that, without some means of calling learners and teachers to reach beyond themselves, beyond the reductionist tendencies of the culture surrounding them, the child-centered classroom may become the self-centered classroom—and this, indeed, furnishes the core of the conservative critique of this approach to education.

We should be clear: Neither "traditionalist" nor "progressivist" classrooms are necessarily or completely dysfunctional. Both these pedagogies do work for some teachers and some students, including some students from minority and working-class cultures. But there is no lack of evidence that the latter are disproportionately disengaged from an educational system where these two pedagogies are the main ones on offer. When cultural mismatches between teacher, student, and curriculum are added to the classroom dynamics, all the potential weaknesses of the system are magnified. Communicative barriers attenuate the I-Thou relationship— the authoritative artifacts of cultural production carry with them deep lessons of arbitrary power and exclusion—and attempts to involve the learner in active inquiry are limited by the school's ability to acknowledge and respond to difference and inequity.

These issues have gradually come to be recognized in that small proportion of educational research that focuses on diversity; but it has not been a straightforward process of discovery. This is because a rather different conception of the problem—not, in its origins, an educational prescription, but rather an idea about culture and identity—has become entrenched in our everyday thinking about schools. People's sense of self-worth, we have come to believe, depends in part on public recognition of their worth, including the value of the cultural group to which they belong. To foster children's attachment to school, including their willingness to learn, schools need to include aspects of their home cultures in the curriculum and in the physical environment of the classroom. Arts and crafts, field trips, festivals, and other means are used to accomplish this objective. So widespread have such practices become that they are sometimes taken to constitute the essence of "multicultural education," along with a general emphasis on tolerance and understanding among all cultures.

The central idea here is an important and valid one, with deep roots in the modern sense of self, as Charles Taylor (1994) has argued. Even at their most superficial ("holidays and heroes," "beads and bannock"), such practices affirm the significance of cultural difference in children's lives. At their best, they can engage children in memorable experiences that help them relate more positively to themselves and to one another, across cultural divides. Yet even in such optimal cases, the multicultural component of the curriculum is almost always seen as separate from, or peripheral to, its academic dimension. Culture is included to make kids feel good and to encourage them to invest more effort in acquiring the high-status, high-stakes knowledge (English, mathematics, science) that school is really about. When culture, in this sense of political representation, does make it into the academic curriculum, it typically loses its connection with children's understanding and becomes one more mystifying stop on the endless tour. (See, for example, Rochelle Gutiérrez's [2000] examination of "multicultural mathematics" in U.S. schools.) The author arrives at a similar conclusion to that of Sonia Nieto (1999), to the effect that "student learning and teacher transformation need to be at the very heart of multicultural education" (p. 163). Curricular change is not enough.

Over the past 40 years, multicultural education has come to recognize all these issues and to develop responses to them. Teachers can be recruited from minority cultures, or educated to be knowledgeable about the ways the latter manifest themselves in the classroom; curricula can be reformed to include knowledge about and from such cultures; student inquiry can be taken outside the classroom into the community; and students' experience can be brought into the classroom for exploration. But what has also become evident is the capacity of the system to absorb such interventions without altering the basic dynamic. Minority teachers can be socialized into rigid, disempowering pedagogies; teachers' ideas about children's cultures and learning styles can be essentialized; "cultural inclusion" can result in curricula as objectified and disengaging as those they replaced; and encounters between school and community can be superficial or alienating. The cultural dynamics of modernity act something like a gravitational field, pulling schools toward a local minimum of cross-cultural engagement, even as visionary teachers and other committed educators push back.

If there is a name for this opposing force, it is imagination. Good multicultural education is education that expands the *imagination* of teachers and learners alike. Good multicultural education fosters schools that reimagine their communities and students who will dedicate their lives to bringing that vision into being. This notion is latent in the literature, but making it explicit may help us to see connections and avoid dead ends. Indeed, it may help us understand that good education, in this interconnected world, is multicultural education: that no less an imaginative effort will do than that which multicultural education calls forth.

## FOUR DIMENSIONS OF IMAGINATION

Following the analysis so far, we can see that education calls on the imagination to expand in at least four directions, or dimensions:

- *the moral dimension*, in which the I reaches out toward the Thou, and whose affective counterpart is *empathy*;
- *the poetic-aesthetic dimension*, in which the I reaches out toward the It, and whose affective counterpart is *wonder*;
- *the social-ecological dimension*, in which the I reaches beyond the I-Thou-It relationship toward the world that encompasses all three, and whose affective counterpart is *hope*;
- and, finally, *the spiritual dimension*, in which the I reaches toward the Self, thought of as that vast ground of our being and knowing that extends beyond the conscious ego. This quest has been part of all the great religious teachings (among which I would include such modern authors as Carl Jung). I have not been able to find an English word that precisely conveys the affective counterpart of the spiritual imagination, but it is best conveyed in the notion of feeling *called to something*, something that makes an exorbitant demand on one's being.

Now, it is not the feelings themselves that are important here: They are simply a way of letting us know that something else is going on, or has the potential to happen. We might call them a sign of the "learnable moment," when the circumstances of our inner and outer worlds coincide. The learning itself may be immediate and almost effortless, or it may be protracted and grueling. It may require no more than the resources we already possess, (deploying them in new ways or for new purposes), or it may require us to acquire new resources (physical or cultural or both). That initial insight, creative spark, shock of recognition, or however we want to characterize the imaginative leap that sets learning in motion, may be perfect and complete, or misleading, or vague, or indeed deeply wrong, based on an understanding of the world that is morally, poetically, aesthetically, socially, ecologically, or spiritually inadequate. Imagination carries no guarantees.

It follows that a theory of education in which imagination is central will not be one that sets modern anxieties at rest. Maxine Greene (1995) sees this clearly: Her pedagogy for "releasing the imagination" would help us "seek more shocks of recognition as the time goes on, more explorations, more adventures into meaning, more active and uneasy participation in the human community's unending quest" (p. 151). For her this quest is very clearly multidimensional. The poetic imagination, the social imagination, the imaginative shaping of one's own life narrative—all these contribute to one's becoming an effective teacher. Her book advocates a lifelong struggle against "the habitual, the taken-for-granted, the unquestioned" (p. 23). And she is quite clear about its relevance to the "passions of pluralism":

> To open up our experience (and, yes, our curricula) to existential possibilities of multiple kinds is to extend and deepen what each of us thinks of when he or she speaks of a community. If we break through and disrupt our surface equilibrium and uniformity, it does not mean that a particular ethnic or racial tradition will, or ought to, replace our own. . . . My point is that we need openness and variety as well as inclusion. We need to avoid fixities, even the stereotypes linked to multiculturalism. (161–163)

This is not a quest with a defined end, or even a single clear direction. The ends emerge through the process of the quest itself. However, to say that an imaginative theory of education is necessarily open ended and incomplete is not to imply that we cannot discover a great deal about how to do it better. One would not expect to come up with foolproof (or teacher-proof) recipes for imaginative engagement and development, but there could well be strategies, approaches, philosophies, that make such development more likely to happen. In other words, it may be pedagogically fruitful to ask how one can better engage the imaginations of one's students, provided that this engagement is conceived of in a sufficiently rigorous way.

Such conceptions may be available in the literature for all four dimensions sketched above, but if so, I am not yet familiar enough with most of them. What I wish to focus on in the remainder of this chapter is some work that has centered, so far, on developing what I have called the poetic-aesthetic dimension of the imagination. The foundations of this approach were laid by Kieran Egan's body of work, to which I have added a more explicit focus on cultural inclusion. While far from complete, the following sketch may serve to illustrate what sustained research into imaginative development may entail.

## THE EDUCATED IMAGINATION: A TRAGICOMIC NARRATIVE

Four themes seem to me to be central in Egan's work, as summarized in his most complete account of this educational theory, *The Educated Mind* (1996):

- an emphasis on the vital role of emotion in thinking and understanding;
- a notion of cultural mediation as progressing in somewhat distinct stages;

- a narrative of imaginative development that entails losses as well as gains;
- a basic optimism about the imaginative potential of teachers.

While each of these themes is shared with some other educational thinkers, the combination is unique.

The affective emphasis was prefigured in the preceding section. That the emotions are centrally involved in thinking is now widely recognized in cognitive science and philosophy, although the full implications are far from being worked out. The division of thinking and feeling, mind and body, is so deeply embedded in Western tradition that it is not clear how far down one must dig into its foundations in order to overcome it. In Andy Clark's (1997) phrase, "Humpty Dumpty is going to take a whole lot of putting together again."

Imagination, then, functions in Egan's work as a kind of Humpty-Dumpty glue, both theoretically and practically. Reconceptualizing teaching and learning to give imagination a central role is a way of ensuring that we do not fall into the old conceptual traps; it also turns our pedagogical attention to precisely those interactions in which heart and head work together.

Egan's concept of cultural mediation helps to make this idea more precise and useful. Philosophically it is allied to Vygotsky's more widely known theory, but it is worked out in quite a different way. For Vygotsky, the acquisition of language produces a fundamental discontinuity in intellectual development: The young child's exploration of the world becomes channeled in the directions favored by the society around it, and henceforth the challenge of education is to help the child explore its way along those channels, primarily by supporting the development of concepts securely grounded in a scientific (or, more broadly, disciplined) understanding of the world. Vygotsky differed from many others, including his contemporary Piaget, in viewing imagination in a positive light; but it was certainly not central to his conception of intellectual development.

Writing a half century later, Egan is less categorical in the developmental roles he ascribes to language and to disciplinary thinking. While he, too, thinks that entry into oral language brings with it a whole new set of tools for understanding the world, he emphasizes the degree to which this transformation relies on embodied forms of understanding, and the limitations of language vis-à-vis immediate experience. Similarly, while he too portrays disciplinary thinking as an advanced stage of intellectual development, it is by no means the greatest educational good identified in his theory. What this good is can only really be understood in the context of his overall developmental scheme; and this in turn will shed light on his views on cultural mediation.

Egan (1997) suggests that five "somewhat distinct" kinds of understanding can be discerned in modern society, beginning with the somatic understanding that each of us gains through our bodily encounters with the world. Even as this is developing, our entry into oral language supplies us with a new wealth of tools for perceiving more distant, abstract, and complex forms of order: what Egan calls Mythic understanding. This is followed, as we begin to gain access to the world of print, by the development of Romantic understanding, and later on, possibly, by the Philosophical understanding characteristic of the disciplines. Yet this stage, too, can be folded into a higher one, which Egan terms Ironic: in essence, a reflexive critical understanding of the strengths and limitations of all our attempts to know the world better.

Sketched like this, such a developmental scheme appears merely progressive, one more variation on the comic themes so prevalent in education. Yet it is vital to note that Egan regards each stage as bringing losses as well as gains. Experience can never be quite so immediate and vivid once we have gained a Mythic sensibility, he suggests; in turn, the power and depth of Mythic thinking will be supplanted by more literal and human-oriented perceptions at the Romantic stage. Philosophical thinking has a weakness for generalization and abstraction that may undermine the joyful concreteness of the Romantic mind, while Ironic understanding can easily slide into a kind of cynical relativism. Thus the educational challenge is to preserve the best features of each stage even as new kinds of thinking are being developed, thereby ensuring that the latter are as energetic and flexible as possible. Only if this can be achieved will the goal be reached of a fully developed and integrated Ironic understanding.

What Egan offers, then, is a tragicomic narrative of education, in place of the merely comic. It is simultaneously a tragicomic view of history, for he suggests that the progression from Somatic to Ironic recapitulates somewhat similar stages of cultural development, with significant losses at every stage: the long-ago leap from ape to language-user, the discovery of writing, the invention of the disciplines, and the growing realization, over the past hundred years, that none of this offers the existential certainty that the founders of modernity hoped it might.

Now this is clearly a perspective founded on Western history, for writing and disciplinary thinking have not played equivalent roles in all cultures. It is thus designed to apply to educational institutions whose task is to instill Western (or, more broadly, modern) traditions of thought in new generations. As such, it will not appeal to those who prefer to condemn the canon in root and branch; but for critics seeking a *modus vivendi* with modernity, it is remarkably hospitable toward alternative cultural histories and modes of thought. Rather like Bakhtin's (1981) notion of *heteroglossia*, of "a multitude of concrete worlds, a multitude of bounded verbal-ideological and social belief systems" contained within a national language (p. 288), Egan's work implies that different kinds of understanding jostle for primacy in the worlds of the classroom, school, and community. Rather than privileging one set of these above all others, his educational scheme enjoins us to treat them all with respect—while nonetheless seeking to develop them further, to draw out their potential for deeper insight into ourselves and our world.

The task of such drawing out belongs to all of us, but teachers must necessarily bear a disproportionate share of the load. Unusually, for work with such a strong philosophical bent, Egan has dedicated considerable attention to the implications of his theory for classroom practice. In works such as *Teaching as Storytelling* (1986), *Imagination in Teaching and Learning: The Middle School Years* (1992a), and the recent *An Imaginative Approach to Teaching* (2005), he suggests ways in which teachers can rework the curriculum to engage and develop their students' imaginations, with a particular emphasis on the fostering of Mythic and Romantic understanding in elementary schools. In 2001 Egan and a handful of colleagues at Simon Fraser University founded the Imaginative Education Research Group to carry forward this work with teachers and teacher educators. The group now offers a master's program in imagination and education, hosts an annual conference for around 400 participants, and is conducting a 5-year collaborative research project with Aboriginal communities and school districts in various parts of British Columbia.

While still at a relatively early stage, this empirical work with teachers and schools has already demonstrated that infusing classrooms with imagination is a more difficult and complex task than it might appear on the surface. Teachers are required to think in unfamiliar ways, to acquire new kinds of resources, to take risks in what they ask of children, and to reexamine their assumptions about children's learning and the roles of community and culture. Such findings bear a striking resemblance to the conclusions of the literature on multicultural education cited earlier. *Curriculum is not enough*: This is the message that should be inscribed in letters of fire on the wall of any imaginative classroom. Indeed, it is our work on implementing Egan's ideas in diverse classroom contexts that inspired the search for a multidimensional framework, capable of articulating the relationship between curricular and other aspects of imaginative education.

## THE IMAGINATIVE MULTICULTURAL PROJECT

It seems plausible that this project, which aims at integrating the moral, poetic-aesthetic, socioecological, and spiritual dimensions of education, can apply some of the hard-won insights of Egan's educational theory in more general ways. The following are some tentative guiding principles derived from the foregoing discussion:

1. Children's understanding is different from that of adults, but no less energetic or internally consistent. Look to what may be lost as well as gained in the process of imaginative development. Study what engages children deeply in particular aspects of the world, sparking wonder, empathy, hope, or longing. Do not seek to rush them too quickly to stages that may seem desirable from an adult perspective; instead, seek out and cultivate the good in every stage.
2. The imagination develops culturally and communally, not just individually. Look to major transitions in the history of the culture for insight into where obstacles may lie and the potential for transformation may be found. Try to understand the vision and motivation of important cultural figures from these times of transition to nurture similar passionate engagement in the children of today.
3. It is probably illusory to suppose that one can work in only one imaginative dimension at a time: the four dimensions described here are intimately involved with one another. Thus curriculum work in the poetic-aesthetic dimension is likely to have (or require) deep moral underpinnings, work on developing children's socioecological understanding may well enhance (or place demands on) their spiritual self-awareness, and so on. For this reason, the implementation of imaginative education may well proceed more smoothly in schools guided by a holistic vision of education, such as those of Rudolf Steiner (Waldorf schools), Gregory Cajete (indigenous education), or Ken Wilber (integral education).
4. There is no getting around the importance of good teaching for imaginative development. Yet such teaching also *entails* the similar development of teachers themselves, in all four dimensions: not all at once, perhaps, but over the long haul. Careful thought must therefore be given to the support and nurturing of such teachers. In this respect it is worth noting a small study of teachers using Egan's ideas in the classroom (McKenzie & Fettes, 2002), which demonstrated the importance of supportive colleagues, administrators, and university collaborators in sustaining a long-term commitment to imaginative teaching.

Many of these principles reappear, in various guises, in the recent research literature on multicultural education. For instance, Sonia Nieto (1999, pp. 130–161) shows how her own graduate students come to understand how their own identities and those of their students are bound up with broader societal relations; Sleeter and Montecinos (1999) contrast two different field experiences intended to promote such understanding; Lesko and Bloom (2000) ... the "ghosts" ... demanded that they open up their tity and experience; Johnson (1992) ecology of a teacher's struggle to classroom. In these and other works, nent is tacitly recognized. If we can nd our conception of multicultural ots to embrace the poetic and the ange may arise.

# References

Abram, D. (1996). *The spell of the sensuous*. New York: Vintage.

Abrams, M. H. (1953). *The mirror and the lamp: Romantic theory and the critical tradition*. New York: Oxford University Press.

Abrams, M. H. (1958). *The mirror and the lamp: Romantic theory and the critical tradition*. New York: Norton. (Original work published 1953)

Allende, I. (1991). Our Secret. In I. Allende, *The stories of Eva Luna*. London: Atheneum.

Alvermann, D. (2001). Reading adolescents' reading identities: Looking back to see ahead. *Journal of Adolescent and Adult Literacy, 44*(8), 676–690.

Ames-Lewis, F. (2000). *The intellectual life of the early Renaissance artist*. New Haven, CT: Yale University Press.

Arendt, H. (1977). *Between the past and future*. London: Penguin.

Arnheim, R. (1969). *Visual thinking*. Berkeley: University of California Press.

Aronowitz, S., & Giroux, H. A. (1985). *Education under siege: The conservative, liberal and radical debate over schooling*. South Hadley, MA: Bergin and Garvey.

Ashcraft, M. (1989). *Human memory and cognition*. Glenview, IL: Scott, Foresman.

Bachelard, G. (1958). *The poetics of space* (Trans. Maria Jolas). Boston: Beacon.

Bailin, S. (1988). *Achieving extraordinary ends: An essay on creativity*. Dordrecht, Holland: Kluwer.

Bailin, S. (1994). *Achieving extraordinary ends: An essay on creativity*. Norwood, NJ: Ablex.

Bailin, S. (2003). Is argument for conservatives: Or where do sparkling new ideas come from? *Informal Logic, 23*(1), 1–15.

Bailin, S., Case, R., Coombs, J. R., & Daniels, L. B. (1999a). Common misconceptions of critical thinking. *Journal of Curriculum Studies, 31*(3), 269–283.

Bailin, S., Case, R., Coombs, J. R., & Daniels, L. B. (1999b). Conceptualizing critical thinking. *Journal of Curriculum Studies, 31*(3), 285–302.

Bakhtin, M. (1981). *The dialogic imagination: Four essays* (C. Emerson & M. Holquist, Trans. and Ed.). Austin: University of Texas Press.

Barbeau, E. (1985). Creativity in mathematics. *Interchange, 16*(1), 62–69.

Barnes, M. (2000). "Magical" moments in mathematics: Insights into the process of coming to know. *For the Learning of Mathematics, 20*(1), 33–43.

Barrow, R. (1988). Some observations on the concept of imagination. In K. Egan & D. Nadaner (Eds.), *Imagination and Education* (pp. 79–90). New York: Teachers College Press.

Barrow, R. (1990). *Understanding skills: Thinking, feeling, and caring.* London, Ontario: Althouse Press.

Barton, D. (1994). *Literacy: An introduction to the ecology of written language.* Oxford, UK: Basil Blackwell.

Barton, D., & Hamilton, M. (2000). Literacy practices. In D. Barton, M. Hamilton, & R. Ivanic (Eds.), *Situated Literacies: Reading and writing in context* (pp. 7–15). London: Routledge.

Barzun, J. (2000). *From dawn to decadence: 1500 to the present.* New York: HarperCollins.

Belio, J. (1970). *Traditional Balinese culture.* New York: Columbia University Press.

Benjamin, W. (1969). *Illuminations* (Harry Zohn, Trans.). New York: Schocken Books.

Bernstein, B. (1971). *Class, codes and control: Theoretical studies towards a sociology of language* (Vol. 1). London: Routledge & Kegan Paul.

Beth, E., & Piaget, J. (1966). *Mathematical epistemology and psychology.* New York: Gordan and Breach.

Block, N. (Ed.). (1981). *Imagery.* Cambridge, MA: Massachusetts Institute of Technology Press.

Boorstin, D. J. (1992). *The creators.* New York: Random House.

Borwein, P., & Jörgenson, L. (2001, December). Visible structures in number theory. *MAA Monthly, 108*(5), 222–231.

Brown, S., & Walters, M. (1983). *The art of problem posing.* Hillsdale, NJ: Lawrence Erlbaum.

Bruner, J. (1962). *On knowing: Essays for the left hand.* Cambridge, MA: Belknap Press.

Bruner, J. (1964). *Bruner on knowing.* Cambridge, MA: Harvard University Press.

Bruner, J. (1977). *The process of education.* Cambridge, MA: Harvard University Press. (Original work published 1960)

Bruner, J. (1986). *Actual minds, possible worlds.* Cambridge, MA: Harvard University Press.

Burton, L. (1984). *Thinking things through.* Oxford, UK: Basil Blackwell.

Burton, L. (1999). Why is intuition so important to mathematicians but missing from mathematics education? *For the Learning of Mathematics, 19*(3), 27–32.

Canadian Centre for Education Alternatives. (1999). *Peer to peer literacy corps: Stage 3.* Funding documentation prepared for Ministry of Advanced Education, Training and Technology, Province of British Columbia. Vancouver, British Columbia: Author.

Casey, B. (n.d.) *Let's play.* BBC Education Online. Retrieved July 18, 2002, from http://www.bbc.co.uk/education/grownups/articles/geneducation/letsplay/printable.html

Casti, J. L. (1989). *Paradigms lost: Tackling the unanswered mysteries of modern science.* New York: William Morrow.

Chambliss, J. J. (1974). *Imagination and reason in Plato, Aristotle, Vico, Rousseau, and Keats.* The Hague, Netherlands: Martinus Nijhoff.

Clark, A. (1997). *Being there: Putting brain, body, and world together again.* Cambridge, MA: Massachusetts Institute of Technology Press.

Cobb, E. (1977). *The ecology of imagination in childhood.* Dallas, TX: Spring Publications.

Codell, E. R. (1999). *Educating Esmé: Diary of a teacher's first year.* Chapel Hill, NC: Algonquin.

Coleridge, S. T. (1816). *Kubla Kahn.* Retrieved November 18, 2002, from: http://www.thecore.nus.edu.sg/landow/victorian/previctorian/stc/kktext.html.

Coleridge, S. T. (1985). *Biographia literaria.* Princeton, NJ: Princeton University Press. (Original work published 1817)

Coles, R. (1989). *The call of stories: Teaching and the moral imagination.* Boston: Houghton Mifflin.

Cope, B., & Kalantzis, M. (Eds.). (2000). Introduction. In *Multiliteracies: Literacy learning and the design of social futures* (pp. 3–8). London: Routledge.

Cornford, F. M. (1941). *The Republic of Plato.* London: Oxford University Press.

Covarrubias, M. (1932). *Island of Bali.* Oxford, UK: Oxford University Press.

Cullingford, C. (1991). *The inner world of the school: Children's ideas about schools.* London: Cassell.

Davis, P., & Hersch, R. (1980). *The mathematical experience.* Boston: Birkhauser.

de Montaigne, M. (1993). *Essays* (J. M. Cohen, Trans.). London: Penguin. (Original work published 1580)

Dewey, J. (1933). *How we think.* Boston: D. C. Heath.

Dewey, J. (1938). *Logic: The theory of inquiry.* New York: Henry Holt.

Dewey, J. (1966). *Democracy and education.* New York: Free Press. (Original work published 1916)

Dewey, J. (1985). *Democracy and education.* In *The middle works* (Vol. 9). Carbondale: Southern Illinois University Press.

Dewey, J. (1987). *Art as experience.* In *The Later Works* (Vol. 10). Carbondale: Southern Illinois University Press.

Diggins, J. P. (1994). *The promise of pragmatism: Modernism and the crisis of knowledge and authority.* Chicago: University of Chicago Press.

Dissanayake, E. (1995). *Homo aestheticus: Where art comes from and why.* Seattle: University of Washington Press.

Egan, K. (1986). *Teaching as story telling.* London, Ontario: Althouse.

Egan, K. (1992a). *Imagination in teaching and learning: The middle school years.* Chicago: University of Chicago Press.

Egan, K. (1992b). *Imagination in teaching and learning: The middle school years.* London, Ontario: Althouse.

Egan, K. (1996). *The educated mind.* Chicago: University of Chicago Press.

Egan, K. (1997). *The educated mind: How cognitive tools shape our understanding.* Chicago: University of Chicago Press.

Egan, K. (2002). *Getting it wrong from the beginning: Our progressivist inheritance from Herbert Spencer, John Dewey, and Jean Piaget.* New Haven, CT: Yale University Press.

Egan, K. (2005). *An imaginative approach to teaching.* San Francisco: Jossey-Bass.

Egan, K., & Nadaner, D. (Eds.) (1988). *Imagination and education.* New York: Teachers College Press.

Eisner, E. W. (1985). *The educational imagination: On the design and evaluation of school programs* (2nd ed.). New York: Macmillan.

Engell, J. (1999). *The creative imagination.* Cambridge, MA: Harvard University Press. (Original work published in 1981)

Felshin, N. (1995). *But is it art? The spirit of art as activism.* Seattle, WA: Bay Press.

Feynman, R. P. (1999). *The pleasure of finding things out.* Cambridge, MA: Perseus.

Fine, M. (1994). Working the hyphens: Reinventing self and other in qualitative research. In N. K. Denzin & Y. S. Lincoln (Eds.), *Handbook of qualitative research* (pp. 70–82). Thousand Oaks, CA: Sage.

Fischbein, E. (1987). *Intuition in science and mathematics: An educational approach.* Dordrecht, Holland: Kluwer.

Freire, P., & Macedo, D. (1987). *Literacy: Reading the word and the world.* London: Routledge.

Frye, N. (1963). *The educated imagination.* Toronto, Ontario: Canadian Broadcasting Corporation.

Furst, L. (1969). *Romanticism in perspective.* New York: Macmillan.

Gaines, R., & Price-Williams, D. (1990). Dreams and imaginative processes: American and Balinese artists. *Psychiatric Journal of the University of Ottawa, 15*(2), 107–110.

Garrison, J. (1997). *Dewey and eros: Wisdom and desire in the art of teaching.* New York: Teachers College Press.

Goodlad, J. (1984). *A place called school: Prospects for the future.* New York: McGraw-Hill.

Greene, M. (1995). *Releasing the imagination: Essays on education, the arts, and social change.* San Francisco: Jossey-Bass.

Greene, M. (2000). *Releasing the imagination: Essays on education, the arts, and social change.* San Fransisco: Jossey-Bass.

Gross, A. G. (1990). *The rhetoric of science.* Cambridge, MA: Harvard University Press.

Gutiérrez, R. (2000). Is the multiculturalization of mathematics doing us more harm than good? In R. Mahalingam & C. McCarthy (Eds.), *Multicultural curriculum: New directions for social theory, practice, and policy* (pp. 199–219). New York: Routledge.

Hadamard, J. (1954). *The psychology of invention in the mathematical field.* New York: Dover.

Hanson, K. (1988). Prospects for the good life: Education and perceptive imagination. In K. Egan & D. Nadaner (Eds.), *Imagination and education* (pp. 128–140). New York: Teachers College Press.

Hawkins, D. (1974). *The informed vision: Essays on learning and human nature.* New York: Agathon.

Hilgenheger, N. (1993). Johann Friedrich Herbart. *Prospects: The quarterly review of comparative education, 23*(3/4), 649–664. Retrieved April 21, 2004, from http://www.ibe.unesco.org/International/Publications/Thinkers/ThinkersPdf/herbarte.pdf

Hirst, P. (1969). The logic of curriculum. *Journal of Curriculum Studies, 1*(2), 142–158.

Hofstadter, D. (1980). *Gödel, Escher, Bach: An eternal golden braid.* New York: Vintage.

Holton, G. (1986). *The advancement of science, and its burdens.* New York: Cambridge University Press.

Hume, D. (1888). *A treatise of human nature* (L.A. Selby-Bigge, Ed.). Oxford: Oxford University Press. (Original work published 1739)

Ihimaera, W. (1987). *The whale rider*. New York: Harcourt Children's.

Jhanji, R. (1988). Creativity in traditional art. *British Journal of Aesthetics, 28*(2), 162–172.

Johnson, L. (1992). *My posse don't do homework*. New York: St. Martin's.

Johnson, M. (1993). *Moral imagination: Implications of cognitive science for ethics*. Chicago: University of Chicago Press.

Kasner, E., & Newman, J. (1940). *Mathematics and the imagination*. New York: Simon & Schuster.

Kearney, R. (1988). *The wake of imagination: Toward a postmodern culture*. London: Hutchinson.

Kearney, R. (1994). *The wake of imagination: Toward a postmodern culture*. London, UK: Routledge.

Keatinge, M. W. (Trans. and Ed.). (1901). *The great didactic of John Amos Comenius*. Kila, MT: Kessinger.

Kemp, M. (1977). From "mimesis" to "fantasia": The quattrocento vocabulary of creation, inspiration and genius in the visual arts. *Viator: Medieval and Renaissance Studies, 8,* 347–398.

Kemp, T. P., & Rasmussen, D. (1989). *The narrative path: The later work of Paul Ricoeur*. Cambridge, MA: Massachusetts Institute of Technology Press.

King, R. (2000). *Brunelleschi's dome: How a Renaissance genius reinvented architecture*. New York: Penguin.

Kristeller, P. O. (1990). *Renaissance thought and the arts*. Princeton, NJ: Princeton University Press.

Krutetskii, V. (1976). *The psychology of mathematical abilities in schoolchildren*. Chicago: University of Chicago Press.

Kuhn, T. S. (1962). *The structure of scientific revolutions* (2nd ed.). Chicago: University of Chicago Press.

Lesko, N., & Bloom, L. R. (2000). The haunting of multicultural epistemology and pedagogy. In R. Mahalingam & C. McCarthy (Eds.), *Multicultural curriculum: New directions for social theory, practice, and policy* (pp. 242–260). New York: Routledge.

Liljedahl, P. (2004). *The AHA! experience: Mathematical context, pedagogical implications*. Doctoral thesis, Simon Fraser University, Burnaby, BC, Canada, 2004.

Luria, S. F. (1986, April). Review of *The transforming principle,* by Maclyn McCarty. *Scientific American, 254,* 24–31.

MacIntyre, A. (1981). *After virtue*. Notre Dame, IN: University of Notre Dame Press.

Mason, J., Burton, L., & Stacey, K. (1982). *Thinking mathematically*. London: Addison-Wesley.

McCarthey, S. J., & Moje, E. (2002). Conversations: Identity matters. *Reading Research Quarterly, 27*(2), 228–238.

McCleary, D. (1993). *The logic of imaginative education*. New York: Teachers College Press.

McFarland, T. (1985). *Originality and imagination*. Baltimore: Johns Hopkins University Press.

McKenzie, M., & Fettes, M. (2002). *Imaginative education as praxis*. Burnaby, BC: The Imaginative Education Research Group, Simon Fraser University.

McLaren, P. (1994). *Life in schools: An introduction to critical pedagogy in the foundations of education*. White Plains, NY: Longman.

McMillan, M. (1923). *Education through the imagination*. New York: D. Appleton. (Original work published 1904)

Mock, R. (1971). *Education and the imagination*. London: Chatto & Windus.

Moloney, S. (2002). *My thoughts*. Unpublished manuscript, Surrey, BC.

New London Group. (2000). A pedagogy of multiliteracies. In B. Cope & M. Kalantzis (Eds.), *Multiliteracies: Literacy learning and the design of social futures* (pp. 9–37). London: Routledge.

Nieto, S. (1999). *The light in their eyes: Creating multicultural learning communities*. New York: Teachers College Press.

Noddings, N. (1984). *Caring: A feminine approach to ethics and moral education*. Berkeley: University of California Press.

Noddings, N. (1995). *Philosophy of education*. Boulder, CO: Westview Press.

Nussbaum, M. C. (1990). *Loves knowledge: Essays on philosophy and literature*. New York: Oxford University Press.

Oakeshott, M. (1989). *The voice of liberal learning*. New Haven, CT: Yale University Press.

O'Brien, D. (1998). Multiple literacies in a high school program for "at risk" adolescents. In D. Alvermann, K. Hinchman, D. Moore, S. Phelps, & D. Waff (Eds.), *Reconceptualizing the literacies in adolescents' lives* (pp. 27–50). London: Lawrence Erlbaum.

Peirce, C. S. (1955). The scientific attitude and fallibilism. In Justus Buchler (Ed.), *Philosophical writings of Peirce*. New York: Dover Publications. (Original work published 1896–1899)

Perkins, D. (1985). Reasoning as imagination. *Interchange, 16*(1), 14–26.

Poincaré, H. (1952). *Science and method*. New York: Dover.

Polanyi, M. (1967). *The tacit dimension*. New York: Anchor.

Polya, G. (1957). *How to solve it* (2nd ed.). Princeton, NJ: Princeton University Press.

Polya, G. (1981). *Mathematical discovery: On understanding, learning and teaching problem solving* (Vol. 2). New York: Wiley. (Original work published 1965)

Ramseyer, U. (1938). *The art and culture of Bali*. New York: Oxford University Press.

Raywid, M. A. (1981). Up from agape. In W. F. Pinar (Ed.), *Contemporary curriculum discourses*. New York: Peter Lang.

Resnick, L., & Glaser, R. (1976). Problem solving and intelligence. In L. B. Resnick (Ed.), *The nature of intelligence* (pp. 205–230). Hillsdale, NJ: Lawrence Erlbaum.

Ricoeur, P. (1976). *Interpretation theory: Discourse and the surplus of meaning*. Fort Worth: Texas Christian University Press.

Ricoeur, P. (1977). *The rule of metaphor: Multi-disciplinary studies of the creation of meaning in language* (R. Czerny, K. Mclaughlin, & J. Costello, Trans.). Toronto, Ontario: University of Toronto Press.

Ricoeur, P. (1978). *The philosophy of Paul Ricoeur: An anthology of his work* (C. E. Stewart & D. Stewart, Eds.). Boston: Beacon.

Ricoeur, P. (1984). *Time and narrative* (K. Mclaughlin & D. Pellauer, Trans.). Chicago: University of Chicago Press.

Ricoeur, P. (1989). The narrative path. In *The later works of Paul Ricoeur.* Cambridge: Massachusetts Institute of Technology Press.

Ricoeur, P. (1991). *A Ricoeur reader: Reflection and imagination* (M. J. Valdés, Ed.). Toronto, Ontario: University of Toronto Press.

Roberts, W. R. (Trans.). (1954). [Aristotle's] *Rhetoric.* New York: The Modern Library.

Rogers, T., & Schofield, A. (in press). Portraits of youth multiliteracies: Exploring narratives of becoming among students in an alternative secondary program. In J. Anderson, M. Kendrick, T. Rogers, & S. Smythe, *Portraits of Literacy.*

Root-Bernstein, R., & Root-Bernstein, M. (1999). *Sparks of genius: The 13 thinking tools of the world's most creative people.* Boston: Mariner.

Rosenau, P. M. (1992). Post-modernism and the social sciences: Insights, inroads, and intrusions. Princeton, NJ: Princeton University Press.

Rota, G. (1997). *Indiscrete thoughts.* Boston: Birkhauser.

Rousseau, J.-J. (1911). *Émile* (B. Foxley, Trans.). London: Dent. (Original work published 1762)

Rousseau, J.-J. (1979). *Émile or on education* (A. Bloom, Trans.). London: Basic. (Original work published 1762)

Rugg, H. (1963). *Imagination* (K. Benne, Ed.). New York: Harper & Row.

Rusbult, C. (2000). *An introduction to design.* Retrieved online November 18, 2002, from http://www.sit.wisc.edu/~crusbult/methods/intro.htm

Ryle, G. (1949). *The concept of education.* London: Hutchinson.

Saramago, J. (1997). *Blindness.* Orlando, Fl.: Harcourt

Schön, D. (1987). *Educating the reflective practitioner.* San Fransisco: Jossey-Bass.

Siegel, H. (1988). *Educating reason: Rationality, critical thinking and education.* New York: Routledge.

Sinclair, N. (2002). The kissing triangles: The aesthetics of mathematical discovery. *International Journal of Computers for Mathematics Learning, 7*(1), 45–63.

Singer, D. G., & Singer, J. L. (1990). *The house of make-believe.* Cambridge, MA: Harvard University Press.

Singh, S. (1997). *Fermat's enigma.* New York: Viking Penguin.

Slattum, J. (1992). *Masks of Bali.* San Francisco: Chronicle Books.

Sleeter, C., & Montecinos, C. (1999). Forging partnerships for multicultural teacher education. In S. May (Ed.), *Critical multiculturalism: Rethinking multicultural and antiracist education* (pp. 113–137). London: Falmer.

Smith, D. E. (1990). *The conceptual practices of power: A feminist sociology of knowledge.* Toronto, Ontario: University of Toronto Press.

Spies, W., & DeZoete, B. (1983). *Dance and drama in Bali.* London: Faber & Faber.

Spring, J. (2000). *American education* (9th ed.). New York: McGraw-Hill.

Sterling, C. (1994, June 22). Arts education means business. *Education Week.* Retrieved on July 18, 2002, from http://www.edweek.org/ew/ew_printstory. cfm?slug=39ster.h13

Street, B. (1995). *Social literacies: Critical approaches to literacy in development, ethnography and education.* New York: Longman.

Surrey School District. (2003). *Ninth annual report of The Improving Student Learning Committee, 2002–2003.* Surrey, UK: School District 36.

Surrey Social Futures. (2005). *Surrey/White Rock Community Impact Profile, 2004.* Surrey, UK: Author.

Sutton-Smith, B. (1988). In search of the imagination. In K. Egan & D. Nadaner (Eds.), *Imagination and education*. New York: Teachers College Press.

Taylor, C. (1989). *Sources of the self: The making of the modern identity*. Cambridge, MA: Harvard University Press.

Taylor, C. (1992). *Multiculturalism and "the politics of difference."* Princeton, NJ: Princeton University Press.

Taylor, C. (1994). *Multiculturalism: Examining the politics of recognition* (A. Gutmann, Ed. and Intro.). Princeton, NJ: Princeton University Press.

Treffers, A. (1993). Wiskobas and Freudenthal: Realistic mathematics education. *Educational Studies in Mathematics, 25*, 89–108.

Turner, A. R. (1992). *Inventing Leonardo*. Berkeley: University of California Press.

Turner, A. R. (1997). *Renaissance Florence: The invention of a new art*. New York: Harry N. Abrams.

Viereck, G. S. (1929). What life means to Einstein: An interview by George Sylvester Viereck. *The Saturday Evening Post*, October 26, p. 17.

Warnock, M. (1976). *Imagination*. London: Faber.

Weiner, R. P. (2000). *Creativity and beyond*. Albany: State University of New York Press.

Weisberg, R. (1993). *Creativity: Beyond the myth of genius*. New York: W. H. Freeman.

Welch, E. (1997). *Art in Renaissance Italy*. Oxford, UK: Oxford University Press.

White, A. R. (1990). *The language of imagination*. Oxford, UK: Blackwell.

Whitehead, A. (1959). *The aims of education and other essays*. New York: Macmillan.

Whittlesea, B., & Williams, L. (2001). The discrepancy-attribution hypothesis: The heuristic basis of feelings of familiarity. *Journal for Experimental Psychology: Learning, Memory, and Cognition, 27*(1), 3–13.

Wordsworth, W. (1807). *Ode: Intimations of immortality from recollections of early childhood*. In *Oxford Book of English Verse* (p. 536). Oxford: Oxford University Press.

Wordsworth, W. (1991). *The prelude* (S. Gill, Ed.). Cambridge, UK: Cambridge University Press. (Original work published 1805)

# About the Editors and Contributors

**Sharon Bailin** is a professor emerita on the faculty of education at Simon Fraser University, Canada, where she has taught courses in creativity, arts and drama education, and curriculum philosophy and theory. She has written extensively on creativity, on critical thinking, and on arts and drama education. Her book, *Achieving Extraordinary Ends: An Essay on Creativity* (1988), was awarded the Canadian Association for the Foundations of Education Book Award. She has done presentations on her work internationally, including in Hong Kong, Singapore, Israel, Italy, Mexico, and England. Dr. Bailin is a past president of the Philosophy of Education Society (of North America).

**Sean Blenkinsop** is an assistant professor of imaginative education in the faculty of education at Simon Fraser University. He has a 20-year history as an educator with a curricular focus on issues of science and the environment both in and out of the classroom. Dr. Blenkinsop has a Ph.D. in education from Harvard University and an M.Sc. from Minnesota State University. He is currently also a codirector of the Imaginative Education Research Group, which can be explored in more depth at www.ierg.net.

**Kieran Egan** is the author of about twenty books, and coauthor, editor, or coeditor of a few more. In 1991 he received the Grawemeyer Award in Education. In 1993 he was elected to the Royal Society of Canada, in 2000 to the U.S. Academy of Education, and in 2001 to a Canada Research Chair. Various of his books have been translated into about ten European and Asian languages. His books include *The Educated Mind: How Cognitive Tools Shape Our Understanding* (1997), *Building My Zen Garden* (2000), *Getting It Wrong from the Beginning: Our Progressivist Inheritance from Herbert Spencer, John Dewey, and Jean Piaget* (2002), *An Imaginative Approach to Teaching* (2005), and *Teaching Literacy: Engaging the Imagination of New Readers and Writers* (2006).

**Mark Fettes** is an assistant professor of education at Simon Fraser University, Canada. His research is focused on systemic and inclusive approaches to educational and social change, particularly those fueled by concerns over ecological sustainability and cultural and social diversity. To this end he has pursued the development of "ecological" approaches to social and educational theory that might strengthen the decision-making capacity of organizations and communities and increase the range of conceivable alternatives to present systems. Exploring the interplay of language, imagination, community, and schooling, his work covers a wide range of fields, including the epistemology and sociology of language, pedagogy and assessment, educational administration, language policy and planning, translation and interpretation. He has collaborated closely with First Nations people from different parts of Canada, and took a leave of absence in the 2006–07 school year to work as assistant director of Haida Education in British Columbia School District 50.

**Peter Liljedahl** is a former high school mathematics teacher and a father of three very energetic children. Currently he is an assistant professor in mathematics education at Simon Fraser University. Dr. Liljedahl's interest lies in creativity in problem solving, numeracy, mathematical engagement, and the professional growth of teachers. To this end, his research is focused on problem solving and its effect on teaching and learning. Dr. Liljedahl's current research projects include the affective impact on students in a problem-solving environment, the reform of teachers' practices in the context of numeracy, and the implication of alternate assessments on teachers' practice.

**Geoff Madoc-Jones** grew up in Wales where he attended Denbigh Grammar School and the University of Wales in Bangor for his B.A. (Hons.) in History. He came to Canada in 1968 and taught both elementary and secondary language arts from 1969 to 1985 in Vancouver and on the Sunshine Coast. Since 1985 he has worked on the faculty of education, initially as a teacher educator, then as a graduate program developer in graduate programs, and finally as a faculty member. During this time he also completed his M.A. and Ph.D. in the area of philosophy, hermeneutics and language arts education. He was subsequently appointed as an assistant professor, and his research interests include hermeneutics, teaching poetry, and the history of literacy. Since 2004 he has been the coordinator of the Ed.D. in educational leadership program. He is married to Jennifer and has three children, Ruth, Gareth, and Sian.

**Andrew Schofield** was a teacher, teacher educator, and school district administrator in his native South Africa during that country's transition to democracy, serving on provincial and national education-policy reconstruction teams. He returned to the classroom in 2001, teaching and researching in an inner-city secondary school, working with at-risk students, and exploring the interaction of narrative constructions of identity, imagination, and youth literacy pedagogy. This work was recognized internationally with the award of the International Reading Association's President's Grand Prize Award for Reading and Technology (2006). His teaching is enriched by a longstanding relationship with the Imaginative Education Research Group.

**Maureen Stout** is an independent researcher, writer, and now realtor, living in Vancouver, Canada. She was most recently a postdoctoral fellow at Simon Fraser University and is a former assistant professor of education at the California State University, Northridge. Maureen has a Ph.D. in education from UCLA and graduate degrees in languages and politics from the University of London and the London School of Economics, respectively. Her B.A. in English is from the University of British Columbia. She is the author of *The Feel-Good Curriculum: The Dumbing-Down of America's Kids in the Name of Self-Esteem* (2000).

**Keiichi Takaya** received his Ph.D. from Simon Fraser University in 2004. His research interest is in philosophical and historical foundations of education. He is a research associate at the Imaginative Education Research Group, and is currently teaching English and education in Japanese universities, including Tokyo Women's Medical University.

# Index